Mama's Girl

Mama's Girl

VERONICA
CHAMBERS

RIVERHEAD BOOKS

NEW YORK   1996

RIVERHEAD BOOKS
a division of G. P. Putnam's Sons
Publishers Since 1838
200 Madison Avenue
New York, NY 10016

Library of Congress Cataloging-in-Publication Data
Chambers, Veronica.
Mama's girl / by Veronica Chambers.
p.   cm.
ISBN 1-57322-030-2 (acid-free paper)
1. Chambers, Veronica.   2. Panamanian Americans—New York (N.Y.)—
Biography.   3. Brooklyn (New York, N.Y.)—Biography.   4. New York
(N.Y.)—Biography.   I. Title.
F129.P35C48   1996
974.7'1043'092—dc20   95-53765 CIP
[B]

Printed in the United States of America
1   3   5   7   9   10   8   6   4   2

This book is printed on acid-free paper. ∞

Book design by Claire Naylon Vaccaro

acknowledgments

All my love to my mother for many, many things, but especially for giving me the blessing to write this book and not minding that I put all of our business on the street.

My most heartfelt thanks to: Tono Ortega; Diana and Buster Richards; Marcus J. Bleecker and the Bleecker family; Stacey Meisel, Esquire, and her Moms and her Aunt Nunu; Arthur and Louise Hillman; Edna Chatmon; Dr. Pat Sharpe; Lorene Cary; Rosemary Bray; Andy Pellet—keep those letters coming!; Dr. Andrea Polans; Joe Wood; Andrea Davis Pinkney; the two N.W.'s—Nicole Wan and Nicky Weinstock; Renee

Michaels and Claire Salvaggio for being there for me always; and to Sandra Dijkstra and the memory of our Joy Luck movie.

A crazy cool convertible car full of thanks to the West Coast posse: Sonja Bolle and Patrick Goldstein, Anna Perez, John Singleton, Cassandra Butcher, Jennifer and Anthony de la Fuentes (*ustedes saben que yo les adoro*), Rita Holm, Kathryn Miller, Brian Siberell and the Connelly crew: Chris, Gretchen, Henry, and Rose.

I know you aren't supposed to talk about people's Mamas, but I wanted to give an extra special shout out to my sister-girlfriend-diva editor and friends: Retha Powers, my double-dutch partner from way back, and her Mamacita; Jennifer Park and her Mama; Caroline Kim and her Mama; Radica Anikpe in London and her absolutely gorgeous Mama. And for the way she slings ink, thank you to the darling, darling Julie Grau and her Mama.

This book is for my grandmothers and great-grands:
Connie and Cecilia, Miss Sue and Flora.
And to all the female ancestors, who are never forgotten.

But I have peeled away your anger
down to its core of love
and look mother
I Am
a dark temple where your true spirit rises
beautiful
and tough as chestnut
stanchion against your nightmare of weakness
and if my eyes conceal
a squadron of conflicting rebellions
I learned from you
to define myself
through your denials.

from BLACK MOTHER WOMAN *by Audre Lorde*

Mama's
Girl

one

Ten years before Air Jordans, I learned to fly. It's like the way brothers pimp-walk to a basketball hoop with a pumped-up ball and throw a few shots, hitting each one effortlessly. Like a car idling before a drag race, there is an invitation, perhaps even a threat, in the way their sneakers soft-shoe the pavement and the ball rolls around in their hands.

As double-dutch girls, we had our own prance. Three of us and a couple of ropes. It had to be at least three girls—two to turn, one to jump. We knew the corners where you could start a good game. Like guys going up for a layup, we started turning nice and slow. Before jumping in, we would rock back and forth, rocking our knees in order to propel ourselves forward; rocking our hips just to show how cute we were. It wasn't a question of whether we'd make it in, we'd conquered that years before. The challenge was to prove how long we could jump. The tricks we would do—pop-ups, mambo, around the world—were just for show, just to work the other girls' nerves. The real feat was longevity. So when we picked the corner where we were going to double dutch, we came with ropes and patience.

There is a space between the concrete and heaven where the air is sweeter and your heart beats faster. You drop down and then you jump up again and you do it over and over until the rope catches on your foot or your mother calls you home. You keep your arms to your sides, out of the way, so they don't get tangled in the rope. Your legs feel powerful and heavy as they beat the ground. When you mambo back and forth, it's like dancing. When you do around the world, it's like a ballet dancer's pirouette. In the rope, if you're good enough, you can do anything and be anything you want.

> *Beverly Road go swinging,*
> *Beverly Road go swing-ing,*
> *Beverly Road go swinging,*
> *Beverly Road go swing-ing.*

On my side of the street is where we jumped rope because Drena, who lived by me, had the best rope, and like cattle, we followed the rope. The best kind of jumping rope was telephone wire because it was light, yet sturdy, and it hit the sidewalk with a steady rhythm—tat tat tat. The telephone wire that connected your phone to the jack was not long enough. The only way to get telephone rope was from someone who worked for the telephone company. Drena's uncle was a telephone repairman so she always had rope.

The worst kind of rope was the kind you bought in the store—cloth ropes with red plastic handles that came in plastic packages with pictures of little blonde girls on them. First of all, they were too short. It would take two or three to make one side of a good double-dutch rope. Second, the ropes were too soft for serious jumping (which only made sense because everybody knew that white girls were no kind of competition when it came to jumping rope). But in a clutch, you could run a soft rope under a hose and get it good and wet to make it heavier. The only problem was keeping it wet.

Miss Mary Mack-Mack-Mack
All dressed in black-black-black
With silver buttons-buttons-buttons
All down her back-back-back

We would split into teams. Only two positions: jumper and turner. You had to be good at both. No captain, just Shannon with her big mouth and Lisa, who really couldn't jump, but talked a lot of junk. With two people turning and one person jumping and everybody else sitting around, waiting for their turn, it wasn't hard to start a fight.

"Pick your feet up! *Pick your feet up!*"

"I hear you."

"Well then, act like it."

"You just mind your business, okay."

Sometimes when I was jumping, I would catch someone on my team yanking the rope so she could call a time-out. Usually, it was Drena because it was her rope and she thought that meant she didn't have to play fair.

"Uh-huh. Start over. Jeanine is turning double-handed," Drena would say. To us, double-handed was something like being crippled or blind. When a double-handed person turned, the ropes would hit against each other, spiraling in lopsided arcs. It not only messed up our jumping, it looked ugly, shaky, and uneven. A good double-dutch rope looked like a wire eggbeater in motion.

"It's okay. It's fine," I would say.

Drena wouldn't be swayed. "Veronica, don't try to cover up. Everybody on the block knows Jeanine is double-handed."

"I am not," Jeanine would mumble.

If there wasn't someone to take Jeanine's place, Drena would wrap up the rope and declare the game over. Then we'd go back to her house and watch t.v. Drena was the only girl on the block to have her own room, plus a canopy bed, a dressing table, a t.v., and a stereo. Staring blankly at *Gilligan's Island,* I would ask Drena, "Why'd you mess up the game? You know Jeanine is not double-handed."

She would roll her eyes. "I'm so sick of those girls. I was just trying to get us out of there." But other times, she would stick to her story and refuse to budge. "You *know* that girl is double-handed. Shut up and pass the Munchos."

> *Ooh, she thinks she's bad.*
> *Baby, I* know *I'm bad.*
> *Ooh, she thinks she's cool.*
> *Cool enough to steal your dude.*

We'd meet at about 3:30, after we'd changed from our school clothes into our play clothes. Then we'd jump until the parents started coming home. Most of our parents worked nine to five in Manhattan and it took them about an hour to get home. We knew it was coming up on six o'clock when we saw the first grown-up in business clothes walking down the hill from the Utica Avenue bus stop.

Sometimes a grown-up woman, dressed in the stockings and sneakers that all our mothers wore for the long commute home, would jump in—handbag and all—just to show us what she could do. She usually couldn't jump for very long. These women had no intention of sweating their straightened hair into kinkiness anyway. But we always gave them props for being able to get down. Secretly, I loved the way they clutched their chests, as if bras were useless in double dutch, and the way their bosoms rose and fell in the up and down rhythm of the rope. I longed for the day I would jump double dutch and have something round and soft to hang on to.

Around this time, I would start looking out for my mother. I could usually spot her from two blocks away. In the spring, she wore her tan raincoat. In the fall, she wore the same raincoat with the liner buttoned underneath. I knew the purses she carried and the way she walked. If I hadn't made up my bed or if I was jumping in my good school clothes, I could usually dash into the house before she got there and do what I was supposed to do. If I was not in trouble, I'd try to make my turn last long enough so that my mother could see me jump.

"Wait, Mom, watch me jump!" I would say. Even though I knew she'd say no.

"I've got to start dinner," she'd say. "And I've seen you jump before."

"But I've learned a new trick!" I'd try not to sound like a baby in front of my friends.

But she wouldn't even turn around. She'd be carrying a plastic shopping bag that held her work shoes and the *Daily News*.

"Some other time," she'd say, closing the gate behind her.

There's so much I can do. So much stuff she doesn't know. But it's always some other time with her.

Here is what I wish she knew: There is a space between the two ropes where nothing is better than being a black girl. The helix encircles you and protects you and there you are strong. I wish she'd let me show her. I could teach her how it feels.

two

My mother never knew her mother. I think about my mommy being motherless and I feel sorry for her, even though she's the parent and I am the child. When I think of her as a little girl, I imagine a little black Orphan Annie. She's explained to me all the arrangements that were made. How she was raised by her grandmother Flora, and her great-grandmother, Miss Sue. How she knew her father, a bartender who worked at a bar called The Blue Room. How when she was little, she would climb the fire hydrant outside and wave at him through the window. She loved her father, she says. She tells me she always felt loved. But I still can't understand how without a mother, any of it would be enough.

Her mother's name was Cecilia. My mother's name is Cecilia, too. There is only one picture of her mother, but I have stared at it a hundred times. She looks just like my mother. They could be twins. They both have the same round face, the same nose, the same expression that's a little tired and a little sad. And I wonder if that's what happens: when a woman dies in childbirth, does she pass on her very same face since she will no longer use it?

"You can't miss what you never had," my mother says.

I don't believe her. My mother is everything. I don't look anything like her. I am darker. My nose is different, my eyes are set closer together, my hair is kinkier, as difficult to detangle as the steel-wool threads of a Brillo pad. If my mother were dead, if she'd died right after having me, if she looked *exactly* like me, then I would more than miss her. I would be obsessed with her. She's living and breathing and I am already obsessed with her.

I ply my mother with questions. I ask to see the picture again and again. In history books, I have seen photographs with that same dark brown glow, like a Polaroid that somebody spilled coffee on. But this photograph is meaningful to me because this woman is my grandmother. Yet because she looks just like my mother, all my life, this photograph always seemed to me a picture of my mother. Like she'd gotten dressed up in old-fashioned clothes for a Halloween party and someone had snapped a shot of her, posing.

"What was her favorite color?" I ask my mother. My

mother rolls her eyes, she thinks my questions are stupid. I am sitting on her bed and going through the big album of photographs from Panama. My favorite color is pink and right now I'm in love with Miss Piggy on *The Muppet Show* because she always wears pink, too.

"I don't know what her favorite color was," she says as she folds a load of towels that just came out of the dryer. I immediately grab the pink towel and press it to my face to feel its soft terry cloth heat.

"What was her middle name?" I ask through the folds of the towel, thinking that this question is a little smarter.

"She didn't have a middle name. It was just Cecilia. Cecilia Roberts," my mother says. There's no emotion in her voice. She could have been talking about Abe Lincoln or some woman she met on the street. How could she not care about her own mother?

Sooner or later, I always ask a certain question even though I know it is the question that will end the conversation.

"Don't you miss her?" I ask. "Didn't you love her?"

My mother turns then and gives me her iciest glare. "Don't you have some homework to do?" she says, in a tone of voice that makes it clear that the answer better be yes. I am dismissed. End of conversation. But I always make myself ask the question, no matter what. It scares me that Mommy could be so cold on the subject of her own mother.

I know what death is and that we all will die, even me.

When relatives would die, my parents would never try to hide what it meant by saying they "passed away" or "crossed over" like other kids' parents did. Dead was dead . . . And I guess what I want to know now is: If I died, like my grandmother had died, would my mother talk about me in that same detached voice? Would she remember that my favorite color was pink and that I carried my lunch in a Miss Piggy lunchbox and that my favorite show was *Charlie's Angels?* Or would she just remember my name and place my photograph in the album with all the other dead people? Would she sit as she did today, calmly folding towels while the borders of my image turned as brown as coffee beans?

Both my parents were born in the Caribbean—my mother in Panama, my father in the Dominican Republic—but my father moved to the States with his family in 1962 when he was twelve years old. My mother's grandmother, Flora, worked in the laundry in the Canal Zone, ironing the American soldiers' pants. She was lucky; she had a pension.

My father joined the U.S. Army after high school and was stationed in Panama. He met my mother and they started dating and soon got married. I was born on the American military base, which made me a United States citizen. My father had joined the civil rights move-

ment and later the Black Power movement. He wanted
to name me Angela Davis Chambers, but my mother put
her foot down and named me after my aunt, Veronica
Victoria. When my little brother was born three years
later, my father got to name him Malcolm X. My mother
had wanted to name him Englebert Humperdinck, after
her favorite singer. That's what she told me.

When I was five years old, my father left the military
and we moved to Brooklyn. First we lived with my father's parents in East New York, then my parents found
an apartment in a two-family house on East 54th Street
in East Flatbush. My mother loved it—it was the biggest
apartment she'd ever lived in and it had a brand-new
kitchen filled with things she'd never seen, like a built-in
oven and a bread bin, and a bathroom with sliding doors.

I went to kindergarten in the public school right
across the street. I loved kindergarten. My mother would
comb my hair into two or three plaits each night and
would lay my clothes out to be ironed along with hers. I
liked dressing up for school. Sometimes I would wear
flared jeans with suede patches—my mother had an out-
fit that was exactly like it. Sometimes I would wear a little
sundress and pretend I was a beautiful lady like my mother
in her long wraparound skirts and high-heeled boots.

But I didn't like the house on East 54th as much as I
liked our next house on Beverly Road. We had the top
floor of a two-family house that had a backyard *and* a

front yard. The kitchen and bathroom were modern and everything worked. There was a room for me and Malcolm to share, a room for my parents, and a room for Flora, who'd come from Panama to live with us.

The house was owned by a strange couple who lived in the downstairs apartment. The wife was definitely in charge. Walking past their door, on my way to school, I could hear her tell him, "Take out the garbage, man. Clean this mess up!"

My mother thought Mrs. Walker was weird because she was the only Jamaican she knew who didn't listen to reggae. Mrs. Walker only listened to classical music. But the music, as lilting and peaceful as it was, was no balm for Mrs. Walker's temper. There was a radio station that my mother listened to as she got ready for work whose slogan was "All news. All the time." That's how I thought of Mrs. Walker, "All screams. All the time."

One day, Mr. and Mrs. Walker had their worst fight yet. Not only was she screaming, but for the first time Mr. Walker was screaming back. We could hear things being thrown against the wall and soon after, the police arrived.

The next day, I went grocery shopping with my mother and as we passed the Walkers' apartment, we saw dried blood on the door. It looked like someone had thrown a whole bottle of ketchup at the door, but I knew it was blood. It had that same dark brown stain that the inside of a Band-Aid had after my mother took it off my scraped knee. "How could he do this to her?" I asked, when we were outside.

"Why do you assume that it is *he* who cut *her?*" she said, pulling me away from the yard where the Walkers might overhear us.

~

It was when we were living above the Walkers that I got to know my grandma Flora. She was really my great-grandmother, but I always just called her Flora. Everyone said she was a big woman—almost two hundred pounds in her best years—and that when she walked the whole building shook. But when Flora came to live with us she was no longer the robust woman my mother had de-scribed. Fat hung off her bones like an oversized dress. She was often ill and took an assortment of pills. The idea was that she would take care of me and my brother after school. But really, we took care of each other. I would open her "safety child-proof" medicine bottles when her hands were too weak. I would bring her water and make sandwiches and keep her company while she watched *novelas,* the Span-ish soap operas, on t.v. She would tell me stories about the carnival in Panama and the *pollera*—the carnival dress she was going to make me so that I could dance on a float.

After Flora came, my father started staying out later and later; hanging out at Brooklyn nightclubs like Ecstasy and Village Hut. He and my mother fought more and more. On Beverly Road, where I thought everything was going to be perfect, things only got worse. When my father hit my mother, I didn't know what to do. Every time he stormed out the door, I thought, I wished, he'd go away for good.

But he would always be back the next day and the two of them would try to pretend that nothing had happened. The pretending set me on edge; I didn't like not knowing what was going on. I would ask my mother and she would say, "It's fine. Don't worry about it." But I couldn't help it. I worried anyway.

After school, I would sit with my grandmother. She would make coffee for herself and tea for me. "I hate the fighting," I would tell her. "What can I do?"

She would look at me sternly. Her eyes, which were blue, always seemed to pop out against her paper-bag brown skin. My mother told me that Flora's grandfather had been a white man. But to me, Flora was unquestionably black.

"Do?" she said. "What do *you* want to do? This is grown folks' business."

Although her voice was strict, there was a sadness in her eyes. I knew she hated feeling powerless as much as I did.

Before I was born, when my mother was a little girl in Panama, there was a man who used to beat his wife. It made Flora so mad because the woman was very tiny.

One day, during a fight, Flora knocked on the door and pulled the man off the woman. While she was holding him back, the woman hit her husband over the head with a big iron pan, knocking him out cold.

When the police finally arrived, the man pressed charges against *Flora* for assault. Flora had to hire a banana-tree lawyer—the Panamanian equivalent of ambulance chasers, so named because they'd climb to the top of a banana tree to look for a case. Luckily, Flora's banana-tree lawyer, a man called Slim, was especially talented and was able to get her out of jail quickly. Flora must have learned that you don't go around butting into married couples' business, not in the 1950s, especially not in Panama where machismo rules.

Hearing all these stories about Flora, I thought that when she moved in, she'd be able to protect my mother, my brother, and me when my father got angry and started to beat us. But there was no fighting back. My grandmother, my mother, and me—we were just women. One old, one only a child, and one somewhere in between. No match for the monster my father would become.

~

When my father announced he was quitting his job at the insurance company, I was outside playing double dutch with my friends. My mother called for me from the house, her face like stone. "Veronica, I need you to come inside," she said. I tried to think of what I could have done wrong and just how much trouble I was in. When I came into the living room, my brother was sitting next to my father. My mother said, "Sit down. Your father has something he wants to tell you."

"I'm going to do my act full time," my father said, smiling.

His office, as we knew, was full of ventriloquist dummies and catalogues and books—books that told you how to perfect illusions, books on great performers like Edgar Bergen and magicians like Houdini and Harry Blackstone. I'd read some of the Houdini books and was amazed at his bravery.

"I think I could be the first really famous black ventriloquist," my father said. "Of course, I won't start making money right from the start. But once I do, I'll be able to buy you all whatever you want."

"Like a Monster Lego set, Daddy?" my brother asked.

"*Ten* Monster Lego sets!" my father said.

I couldn't think of toys. My mother's hands were clenched together and her eyes were wet with tears. There was something bad about this, something she wasn't telling us.

"Okay, children," she said, standing up. "Let's eat dinner."

At first, I loved it when he'd come home and show

us the new routine. The living room would be trans-
formed into a backstage dressing room. There were little
costumes for the dummies, little wigs, and props. There
were the top hats and canes and tuxedos that my father
wore. Sometimes he had matching outfits made for him
and the dummies. Even though we weren't allowed to
touch the clothes and the dummies, we were infected by
my father's excitement. It felt like show biz.

But the more shows my father did, the more he
began to disappear. He would leave for his shows in the
evening and sleep all day. When we came home after
school, he would give us a list of chores to do and then
leave for "meetings." At night, he'd shower, change into
one of his tuxedos, and he'd be gone again.

In the beginning, he drafted my mother to act as his
assistant. She worked as a secretary all day, but he expected her to spend the evenings out, too. My mother
hated wearing the skimpy costume of purple scarves and
gold sequins, but I thought it was the most beautiful
thing. She hated the costume, the stupid lines she had to
recite, the late nights, and the smoky clubs. A couple of
months later, she quit.

All of our chores began to revolve around his act, and
what was at first fun, I grew to hate. My father put together these promotional brochures which consisted of
an 8 X 10 color photo of him and a dummy in black tie,
letters of recommendation from different corporations

and families he had performed for, and a brief biography. My brother and I had to assemble the packets on the living-room floor, assembly-line style.

"I need a hundred folders by Friday," he'd say on a Wednesday afternoon.

We would spend all Thursday afternoon working inside. If in trying to work quickly we made mistakes, he would get furious.

"The staples are on the wrong side!" he would yell. Sometimes if I wasn't paying close attention, my brother would staple the pages on the right side, instead of the left.

"Do you know how much these pictures cost me!" he would scream, ripping packets apart.

In his kinder moments, he would promise us allowances that would never materialize. When I would ask him for the money, he would smile and say, "You should do it for love." But I didn't know if I loved him anymore. I didn't feel like I *knew* him anymore. The fights between him and my mother had only gotten worse. My father had adopted a theatrical, snide attitude that made the usual arguments and beatings seem almost sadistic.

❧

There was an old West Indian rhyme that my father liked to say out loud with me and my brother. He would go: "Children! Children!"

And we would say, "Yes, Papa."

"Where you been?"

"To Grandmama's."

"And what did she give you?"

"Bread and cheese."

"Where's my share?"

"Up in the air."

"How shall I reach it?"

"Climb on a chair."

"What if I fall?"

"We don't care!" we'd scream, and run away as fast as we could. Sometimes after days and days of getting in after we'd gone to bed and getting up after we'd gone to school, my father would try to capture our attention with this rhyme. My brother would join right in, collapsing into giggles at the end. I couldn't believe my father thought that reciting such a silly rhyme could ever, ever be enough. I would mutter my lines until I couldn't say them at all. My father would stop the game short, turning to ask me why I wasn't reciting my lines. Then one day, I stared him down and told him, "Climb on a chair. I don't care." Then I waited to die—either by God striking me down for my insolence or my father beating the life out of me. Neither happened. I walked away, amazed, thinking that he hadn't hit me because he knew I was right. He was a lousy father and no silly rhyme could make me think differently.

Still, there were times when my father could win me over. He began to bring home lots of new music from the clubs. When I was ten, he played us "Rapper's Delight," the first big rap hit. My brother, who was seven, loved the album as much as I did and we played it again and again, trying to memorize the words. "Hip to the hop, you don't stop, rapping to the bang bang boogie . . ." All our friends thought we were so cool to have a copy of the album before anybody else did. They thought it was especially cool that my dad had gotten it for us. We did, too.

❧

What money my father made from the act, he "reinvested" back in the business, buying bigger and better dummies and props. Over dinner, my mother would talk about what bills were due, what was overdue, and what was on the verge of being cut off. I knew my mother paid the bills all on her own. "If it wasn't for me," she would say, "we'd be sitting in the dark. No light. No phone. No gas. Eating air pudding and nothing pie."

Part of me liked it when my mother and father argued over the dinner table, ignoring my brother and me completely. I didn't like to hear them fighting, but I did want to know what was going on. Because the thing is, I knew from the fights I saw and the ones I overheard through the wall at night, that *something* was going on. It felt like anything could happen, anytime. My father could leave. My mother could get so mad at my father, she could leave us. We might move again. Anything could happen. I was always trying to stay on top of the situation, so that when things changed, for better or worse, I would be prepared.

~

My father and mother are arguing in the car. My brother and I are sitting in the back seat. My mother keeps saying over and over, "I just can't take it anymore. I just can't take it anymore." We are driving from Manhattan to Brooklyn and when we are halfway over the bridge, my father pulls the car over and throws it into park.

"If you can't take it anymore, then jump!" he growls, and reaches across her, grasps the door handle, and throws the car door open.

My mother gets out of the car and slams her door closed. My father gets out of the car and slams his door closed. I don't move. The windows are rolled up and I don't dare roll them down. I look out the window and see that my mother is crying. Malcolm doesn't seem to know that we are pulled over on a bridge and that something is very wrong. I don't want to scare him, but I don't know what to do. I know that my father, when he is ready, can beat my mother up and nobody will stop him. I wonder if he will throw her over the bridge. Then I wonder what will happen to us. Will I have to live with my father? Would my aunt raise us? All of a sudden, my mother opens the car door and gets in. My father gets in. We drive home.

∾

My father is seeing another woman. I know because I hear my mother telling one of her friends over the phone. My father travels everywhere with his beeper. Like the props in his act, it's one of his gadgets. It's become his exit line, "I'm gone. Beep me."

Every Saturday morning, my mother would do a thorough cleaning of the house. She'd clean the oven and the refrigerator, mop the bathroom, and vacuum the living room. One morning, I get up from the cartoons I've been watching and go into the living room to ask my mother if we are going to visit my cousins today. My mother has been cleaning the glass coffee table. The bottle of Windex and a roll of paper towels are on the floor. My father's beeper is on the table. My mother is holding a hammer above her head, ready to smash the beeper and the table to pieces. All of a sudden my father appears and sees what she's about to do. He runs over to her screaming, "What, are you crazy? Do you know how much that beeper cost me?" Then he grabs the hammer from her hand and swings it at her head. He hits her with one sure stroke, like he is John Henry and my mother's head is a railroad spike. I am mute. I don't cry.

I think I am dead. I must be dead and I must be in hell. Where else would I see something like this? He will kill her, but all I think about is: She can't leave me alone with him. I love her, but I do not help her. It all happens so fast. The hammer is pure steel and it does not take long to do its cruel work. If it was something else, something softer he was hitting her with, maybe I would have run downstairs to the neighbors. Maybe I would have called 911. It is a moment I will play over and over in my mind. I know now that faced with calamity, I am ineffective.

When the hammer connects, my mother doesn't scream. Her head is gouged. My father sits in the burgundy reclining chair as if he is about to watch his favorite television show. He raises the footrest and crosses his legs. My mother sees me watching and tells me to go to my room, she is going to the hospital. She says it in a calm, grown-up, don't worry voice. But I'm not a fool. I can see the blood. I refuse to move. My father does not offer to drive her. At last I find my voice and beg my mother to take me with her to the hospital. I don't want to be alone with my father. He could kill me while she's gone. She tells me again to go to my room.

Instead, I follow her to the bathroom where she

grabs a towel. She presses the towel against the hole in her head. The towel is white, which she isn't thinking about as she bleeds into the snowy terry cloth. The blood seeps through slowly and the towel turns red in a wavy circle that extends beyond my mother's hand. My mother grabs her purse off the kitchen table and goes out the front door. She's bleeding so much, but she doesn't cry. I run into my grandmother's room and look out the window. I watch my mother walk down the steps. She opens and closes the gate and then she walks away. I watch her for blocks until she turns a corner and then she is gone. I pray harder than I have ever prayed that she comes back, that she isn't so fed up that she turns the corner and keeps on walking.

Just after my mother leaves, my father becomes affectionate. He calls to me from his reclining chair, "Come over and give me a kiss." I look at my father and I meet hate for the first time. By showing me his very worst side, my father introduces me to the worst in myself. Before, I was always scared and helpless because I was a little girl. Now I want to kill him and though I know I can't do it, the desire to hurt him makes me feel stronger. I do not give him a kiss. I go into the bedroom and watch cartoons with my brother.

three

The first Saturday after my father left, my mother woke me and my brother early. It was the day before New Year's Eve. "Let's go," she said, as she led us each into the shower. "I've got some errands to run."

My brother scrunched up his face while standing firmly in place. "Errands?" he said, doubtfully. "Like what?"

My mother started to look vexed, but then smiled. "I'm the mother and you're the child. I don't have to answer your questions. I'm going out. Period. If you want to stay home, stay home."

Inside I was doing somersaults. If Malcolm wanted to

stay home and watch t.v. with Flora, all the better for me. I hardly ever got to go anywhere alone with my mom. Even errands sounded thrilling. Something had happened after my father left. As sad as my mother had been, as scared as she still was, there was suddenly space and light in our house. It was like anything could happen because my father wasn't there. All the rules had changed.

My mother and I got dressed. Before we left, my mother went into the bedroom to talk to Flora. She started speaking quickly in Spanish so I couldn't understand. I walked over to the television where my brother was sitting, two inches from the screen. I took a big bite out of the apple I was eating, then opened my mouth so my brother could see the chewed-up food inside.

"Bleeeeech," I growled, pretending like I was about to throw up all over him.

"*Maaaaa!!!*" my brother screamed. "Vicki is chewing up her food and . . ."

My mother turned around and rolled her eyes. "Enough already," she said to my brother. Then, to me: "Come on, little girl. Let's go."

The minute we got out the door, I asked my mother where we were going. "To the grocery store?" I asked. "To the butcher? To the fish market?"

"Flatbush Avenue" was all she would say.

"But Flatbush Avenue is the biggest street in Brooklyn!" I said, pressing for more details.

"I know," my mother said with a grin. "Now let it rest."

We walked for what felt like miles. I kept thinking I would see one of my friends from school and I could introduce them to my mom, but it was too early in the morning. The only people out were women doing their morning shopping and really little babies being pushed in strollers. Still, I was happy to be hanging out with my mom. Even if it was nine o'clock in the morning.

"This is it," my mother said, stopping in front of what looked like an old Hallmark store.

"A card store?" I asked. "We came all this way to buy a birthday card? They sell cards right down the block from our house. . . ."

"Veronica," my mother said, using the name she reserved for putting me in check. "Shut up."

I walked into the store and surveyed the three or four racks of dusty old cards. There wasn't much of a selection. Why did we come all this way when there were better cards right down our street? I turned to ask my mother, but she had walked to the back of the store where an old Puerto Rican woman sat behind a counter.

"May I help you?" the woman said in English with a heavy accent.

"*Estoy buscando algo para limpiar la casa,*" my mother replied.

Immediately, the woman relaxed. It was a scene I had

witnessed many times before. Latinos would look at my mother's black skin and brush her off. Then, when she began speaking Spanish, their attitude would change. I knew, from my little Spanish, that *"limpiar la casa"* meant "clean the house," but why had my mother come to a card store for Mop & Glo?

I walked up to the counter and looked around. There were all kinds of candles in every color—red candles with hearts on them and the word "Amor" printed across them, white candles and orange candles, rainbow candles and black candles with skulls and crossbones on them like a poison label. There were bottles of different-colored oils, and as the woman began pouring some into little bottles for my mother, I fell in love with the smells. I read the names on the little bottles and they all seemed exotic and exciting: Sage, Roses, Success, Prosperity, Almond, Showers of Gold. By the time we left, my mother had a big shopping bag full of things.

"What do you do with all this stuff?" I asked.

"You'll see," she said.

That afternoon, I watched my mother "clean house" for the first time. She burned incense—frankincense and myrrh. As I read the label I could hardly believe that this was the same frankincense and myrrh I'd read about in the Bible with the three Wise Men. I watched my mother mix up the oils in the bucket and mop the whole house until the scent of incense and oil filled every room. There was a deliberate way in her motions that made me think that even though she saw me, she didn't really see me. She was in her own world. Then it occurred to me that it was like that shampoo commercial, "I'm going to wash that man right out of my hair." My mother was mopping my father right out of the house.

The next night was New Year's Eve and we were all going to a party at one of my mother's friends. But before we went to the party, my mother told us we each had to take a bath. Immediately, my brother started crying. He was going through a big anti-water phase.

"Here we go," my mother said, sighing. "Let's get this over with."

But when my mother stepped toward him, my brother made a mad dash for the living room. My mother ran after him. They stood, facing each other down on either side of the glass coffee table. My mother couldn't reach across and grab him, the coffee table was too wide. She'd always warn us not to play near the table or the glass top might cut us or fall off and break. But now my brother was walking around the coffee table, slowly. My mother started following him, slowly. Then he started to run. She started to run, too. They had gone around two or three times when my mother burst out laughing. Malcolm and I started laughing, too.

"*Fine then!*" she said, laughing harder than I'd ever seen before. "*Stink* up the whole party if you want to."

Then she turned to me. "Come on, Vicki. You first."

I was surprised when my mother followed me into the bathroom. "I can take my own bath," I said, feeling like she was invading my privacy.

"I know," my mother said. "Just call me when you're about to get out of the water."

I filled the tub with water, so hot I could barely stand it, and poured six capfuls of bubble bath instead of the two that the package said I should use. I lay back into the suds and promptly began daydreaming about all the things I would do in the new year. Before long, there was a knock on the door.

"Are you ready?" my mother said.

"I guess so," I answered, with just a little bit of attitude.

My mother didn't notice. She came into the bathroom with a silver basin filled with a mixture of the same water and oils she had used to mop the floor.

"That didn't come from the bucket you used on the floor, I hope," I said, scornfully.

"No," she said, shaking her head. "Why would I do something like that?"

I hadn't noticed the plastic bag in my mother's left hand. But when I saw it, I couldn't figure out why she was bringing a bouquet of white daisies into the bathroom.

"What's that for?" I said, pointing at the bag.

"You'll see." Then she proceeded to pick the petals off the flowers and throw them into the basin. It was like seeing my mother as a little girl for the first time, sitting on the bathroom floor, making daisy chains.

"Ooh, let me have one!" I said, reaching for a daisy. "I want to do He loves me, He loves me not."

Again, she gave me a curious stare. "That's not what I'm doing." She knelt next to the tub. "These oils are for a New Year's blessing. The white flowers are for purification, cleansing. Do you understand?"

Then she began to cup the mixture with her hand and pour it over my head. I jumped at the coolness of the water, but I didn't say a word. For once, I had nothing to say. It felt like I was being baptized, even though I was ten years old. It felt like I was sitting under a waterfall in Hawaii, even though I was just sitting in an old tub in Brooklyn. I felt the water run down my shoulders and back, and as she poured the mixture over me, petals stuck in my hair. I had petals all over my arms and chest. It was strange and amazing and fun.

"Wow," I said, swirling the petals around my bath-water.

My mother got up and turned around to leave. "Don't be long," she said. "Whether he likes it or not, that little boy is going to bathe."

I sat there for a few more minutes with a bouquet of daisy petals blooming like water lilies around me. Although I did not really understand what the bath was about, I did know that things were going to be okay without my father. My mother, as mysterious as she was, would take care of me. I flicked the petals off me, one by one. She loves me. She loves me.

∽

My brother hadn't been able to accept that my parents were getting divorced. He begged my father to stay, while in my head, I kept praying the man would leave. I wanted my father out. If he was gone, I figured the yelling and the screaming and the hitting would stop. Almost all of my friends lived only with their mothers, so I didn't think it was a big deal. But my brother idolized my father and no matter how violent my father became, my brother forgave him. To my brother, my mother was strict and unfair. My father was the one you could always coax into saying yes. I knew that it was my mother who bought the food, the clothes, the school supplies. I knew that just because my father said yes, it didn't mean he'd come through. And while sometimes I would get caught up in his charm, it was my mother I trusted. It was my mother I wanted to stay with.

But when my father told our landlord on Beverly Road about the divorce, the landlord said we had to move out. My mother had been steadily and responsibly paying the rent, but the landlord said, "Mr. Chambers is my friend. If he's not here, you can't stay here either." I loved that house—I loved Beverly Road, loved the tool-shed where we played on rainy days and the blossoming tree in the front yard. When I read *A Tree Grows in Brooklyn,* it was that tree I saw in my mind.

Moving was something I hadn't expected. I thought my father would leave and we would live happily ever after. But it wasn't that simple. Until I was ten, three things were true: We always had a car. We always had a house with a backyard. We always lived with my father. When he left, no matter how glad I was to see him go, it seemed we lost everything in one fell swoop.

It was winter when my father began moving out, though he would continue to drop by for months afterward. "I'll come visit," he would say. "Nothing changes between us." But having to engage in polite conversation with him was so hard for me when all I really wanted to say was, Just go. Be gone already.

Malcolm, my mother, and I started to spend our Saturday afternoons looking for apartments. My mother would bundle my brother and me up in sweater on top of sweater, coats and scarves and hats. We would walk up and down different streets looking for signs that said, Apartment for Rent.

"I can't afford to pay a real-estate agent," my mother explained to me. "As it is, I can barely come up with one month's rent and a month's deposit for the new place."

"We'll find something, Mommy," I said, hoping to sound reassuring and grown up.

As cold as it was, I loved these Saturday outings. I liked being with my mother and helping her look for signs. My brother thought the walks were for the sole purpose of making snowballs. "Behave!" I would say, trying to pinch him through his coat. But as stressed-out as she was, my mother never lost her temper with him.

ॐ

After we moved into the apartment on Ocean Avenue, I began to realize how many things there were that I never knew about my mother. Like the way she went to the religious store to buy incense, candles, and oils. How did she know where to go? What to ask for? I could tell she'd been there before, but I'd never seen any of those little bottles of oil or candles in our house on Beverly Road. How quickly it became apparent to me that I didn't really know my mother at all. For that matter, I didn't really know myself or my brother apart from my father. I thought of everything in terms of what he did and didn't do, what he did or didn't like. Now he was gone and it was like the moment after an eclipse when the sun seems to shine as if for the very first time.

Religion was one of the biggest changes in our life. My father wasn't religious, so we hardly ever went to church. One night after we'd moved into the new apartment, my mother came into our bedroom and said she wanted to teach me and my brother something. She had a Bible in her hands and I wondered where it came from. It was a big black Bible. The only holy books we'd had around the house were the little pocket-sized copies of the New Testament that the church ladies handed out on the street.

My mother sat on my brother's bed. I sat on her left. My brother sat on her right. Oh goodie, I thought. She's going to read to us. My brother and I could read for ourselves, but still I leaned my head on her shoulder and waited silently as she flipped through the pages.

"This is the Twenty-third Psalm," my mother said in a schoolteacher voice I'd never heard her use before. "It's a good prayer."

My brother jumped to his feet, then knelt beside the bed. "I know how to pray! Now I lay me down to sleep, I pray the Lord my soul to keep. If I should die before I wake, I pray the Lord my soul to take."

My mother smiled and pulled him back onto the bed and into her arms. "That's very good, but this is a more

mature prayer. I want you and your sister to memorize it."
Then she closed her eyes and said it softly.

"The Lord is my shepherd; I shall not want.
He maketh me to lie down in green pastures: he lead-
eth me beside the still waters.
He restoreth my soul: he leadeth me in the paths of
righteousness for his name's sake.
Yea, though I walk through the valley of the shadow
of death I will fear no evil, for thou art with me;
thy rod and thy staff, they comfort me.
Thou preparest a table before me in the presence of
mine enemies; thou anointest my head with oil; my
cup runneth over.
Surely goodness and mercy shall follow me all the days
of my life: and I will dwell in the house of the Lord
forever."

My brother and I just looked at each other.

"What was that about?" I asked her.

"It's a good prayer to say when you're scared," my
mother said. "I won't always be with you, but I want you
to know that God is always there."

I tried not to cry, but I could feel the tears coming
up. "*Where* are you going?"

My mother, who hardly ever hugged us, took my
hand, holding it in both of hers. It felt odd because I

couldn't tell if she was hanging on to me or if I was hanging on to her. "I'm not going anywhere," she said. "But it's just us now, and I want you to learn this prayer because you're going to have to be very grown-up from now on."

We practiced saying it a few more times and my mother said we would say it every night until we knew it by heart. "Sometimes when I'm coming home from work," she explained, "the train stops in the middle of the tunnel and the lights go out. You can hear people saying it under their breath. All sorts of people, all with different accents, saying the same prayer. You'll be glad you know it."

∾

Our apartment on Ocean Avenue was different because for the first time we were living in an apartment building with over a hundred other families. With my father, we'd always lived in two-family houses with backyards. Our old neighborhoods were quiet residential areas with houses on every block. This was one brick mass in a sea of brick buildings and there was noise day and night.

It was a tougher neighborhood than I was used to and it took me a long time to get used to girls jumping in my face and boys pulling knives on each other every day after school. It wasn't like I didn't know how to give attitude. In second grade, my friends and I would practice cutting our eyes at each other—staring each other down, then closing our eyes and whipping our heads in the other direction. The gesture had a precise message: *I see you. Now I don't see you. You are* nothing.

Learning how to suck our teeth was an important art to master. A tribute to our West Indian heritage, we would let our mouths fill with spit, then suck it back into our teeth, producing a low but unmistakable hissing sound. Those of us who were the most gifted at this could hiss in long extended notes like a snake or a reedy saxophone. But on Beverly Road all of that was just like jumping double dutch, something else to show off. On Ocean Avenue, it was for real. The wrong look, sucking your teeth at the wrong person, meant a fight. So I tried to stay out of the bullies' way.

Despite the fact that the kids were tougher, I loved school. Since second grade, I was put in accelerated classes. In elementary school, they were called IGC—Intelligent and Gifted Children. It was the first time I'd been singled out for anything, the first time that anyone had said I was special. I was so excited the day I brought the letter home. I could hardly wait for my mother to come home from work. I was outside, jumping rope with my friends, but the minute I saw her walking from the bus stop, I ran up to meet her.

"I've got the best news! I've got the best news!" I squealed.

"Okay, Vicki," she said, sounding like she didn't care. "Give me a chance to get inside and take these shoes off."

Drena and Jeanine needed me to turn for them, but I told them I didn't want to play anymore.

"Don't be like that, Veronica," Drena said. I knew she was pissed. "Wait till you need somebody to turn."

"Sorry," I said, closing the front gate behind me. "See you later."

I went inside and my mother was sitting in the kitchen in her stocking feet, chopping cucumbers for a salad.

"I took this test, right? And they said I was really smart, right?" I sputtered, so excited I could barely get the words out of my mouth. "It's IGC. Intelligent and Gifted Children."

"That's nice," my mother said, but her voice was flat, lifeless.

"Did you *hear* me?" I screamed.

"As long as you pass, whether it's with an A or a C, that's all that matters," my mother said.

I just stared at her. I couldn't believe it. But it was the way she always was. My mother always downplayed achievement, especially as my brother started school and began to do badly. I knew she was trying to make sure there was no competition between us, but I hated it that she ignored all the things I was good at. It was like the less she made of grades, the more important they became to me. I was gifted and intelligent! I got stars on the board in school! If my mother insisted on *pretending* that it didn't matter how good I was in school, then fine.

What confused me about my mother's attitude was this: my ability to read well and read fast was the one thing that my mother and I shared. My aunts and uncles had always told me about how smart my mother was, how as a girl in Panama, she spoke Spanish, French, and English. I knew that Flora loved to read, too. When she came to Panama from Martinique in the 1920s, she had taught herself English by following the subtitles in the movies. Flora loved reading picture-book westerns and comic books. There were piles and piles of comic books in the one-room apartment that my mother and her seven brothers and sisters grew up in. "We didn't have toys," my mother would say. "Reading was the only thing we were allowed to do all day, any time of the day."

My mother took me to get my first library card when I was six. Malcolm was three and had to stay home because he was too little. This alone was reason to celebrate. Perfect summer days would begin with a walk to the Pitkins Market to buy all the food from "back home"— salt fish and sugar cane and fresh mangoes. We would stop by the Jamaican store to get hot beef patties as a snack, then stop at the library to pick up a couple of books on the way home. My mother loved mysteries and humor writers like Erma Bombeck. I started with Beverly

Cleary, then worked my way up to Judy Blume and Paula Danziger. For my mom, reading was something you did for fun. She liked the fact that I read so much because it kept me out of her hair.

In my special class, the teachers often spoke of college. And on t.v. one day, there was a program about students at Harvard University, which was described as one of the best schools in the nation. I loved the way the campus looked, the way the students looked. I wanted to be in a place like that. "Mom, come here," I called from the bedroom. I pointed at the screen—the green lawns, the red brick buildings, the kids in preppy clothes. "That's where I want to go to college," I announced.

My mother turned away from the t.v. slowly and looked at me sternly. "Who has money for that? You should think about going to Brooklyn College."

Brooklyn College? My aunt and some of my cousins had gone there. Our teachers told us it was one of the best colleges in the City University system. But I wasn't impressed. Because of overflow, the sixth-graders in our school attended classes on the Brooklyn College campus. For the six months I was in Girl Scouts, the troop met in a Brooklyn College classroom. I already knew all I needed to know about Brooklyn College. No matter how great a school it was, Brooklyn College would always be in Brooklyn.

I knew that my mother had wanted to go to law

school, but there was no money, no scholarships to help her. I knew from my teachers that if I did well, I could get the money to go. My brother, in comparison, was the only person I ever met who almost flunked kindergarten. He was smart—eventually he would test better in math than I did—but was badly behaved. As he got older, his behavior got worse, until it reached the point where he was always talking back to the teachers and never bothered to do any of the work.

My brother became the subject of much of my mom's worrying. Especially when she got together with her friends. In her own apartment, my mother had begun to have women friends over for the first time. She'd never had anyone visit when we lived with my father, only family. On a Saturday or Sunday, in the late afternoon after the houses were cleaned and the food was cooked, the women would arrive. The doorbell would ring and I would rush to open it.

"Who is it?" I would say.

"It's Esmerelda," a woman might say. Or Marisol. Or Yvonne and Delores. They would answer back with accents so sweet they almost sounded like they were singing. All of my mother's friends were from Panama or the islands.

They would come through the front door wearing the "home clothes" that my mother wore on weekends—house dresses in splashy tropical prints, shorts and

T-shirts and other casual wear in loud colors. Their hair would be dutifully curled in rollers and covered with big silk scarves—never the cloth bandannas that American women wore.

"Wa-pin?" they would say if they were Panamanian. It was shorthand for "What's happening?" and with that phrase, they would make themselves at home. My mother would offer them sorrel or ginger beer if we had any, and they would sit at the dining room table, their conversation weaving quickly in and out of Spanish. They would talk about friends from home and friends who were in Brooklyn with equal passion, as if Brooklyn were only an extension of Panama, a suburb that was just a train ride away.

"But you know that Gabriella's husband has taken up with *esta mujer* and Gabriella is going with the *tramposa*'s husband now?"

"*Sí, manita*. I already heard."

They called each other *"manita,"* which was short for *"hermanita,"* or "little sister," and it seemed like they called my mother this more often than the other way around. My mother was the youngest child in the family, and among other women, my mother often played the younger role. She was quiet, listening more than she talked.

I liked to listen to the women, though it aggravated me that I couldn't understand their Spanish. But I especially hated it when they started talking about their children because it was so clear that the boys were the prize.

"My son Ernesto was just elected student body president," Delores would say, smiling. "*Fíjase, mi'ja.* Maybe he might be president of the country one day. He's born here. It could happen."

I knew Ernesto. We had to see him on various holidays and my mother forced me to go to his birthday parties every year. He was an idiot. If he was student body president, it was only because nobody else wanted to do it. Anytime Delores bragged about him, I kept expecting my mother to jump in and start bragging about me. But she never did. Even though my grades would leave stupid Nesto in the dust.

"He's so smart!" my mother replied sweetly. "I don't know what to do about Malcolm. I got another call from school today. The principal says he's smart. He scores high on the IQ tests, but he doesn't try. And rude! *No me digas.*"

Then Esmerelda would put her two cents in. "He misses his father, *manita,*" she would say. "Boys need their fathers."

"I know," my mother would say. "I know."

There was never any talk about me or what I needed. I was just a quick rest stop in their marathon conversations.

"And Veronica?" they would say eventually.

"She's fine. All A's as usual," she would say. And I could tell from her voice that she was sad, thinking about

Malcolm. She never used the proud, bragging tone that Delores did when she spoke about Ernesto.

I almost would have preferred if they just ignored me altogether. Esmerelda would take it upon herself to start bossing me around. She never called on my brother to do anything, because like most Panamanian women, she thought housework was a girl's domain.

"Veronica!!!" she would scream, even though the apartment was only so big. And most of the time I would be sitting behind the kitchen door eavesdropping, as she well knew.

"Yes," I would say politely. My mother hated it when I said, *Yeah?*

"Come take these glasses and put them in the sink. You've got to start helping around the house now. You're a big girl and your mother could use a break," Esmerelda would go on and on. She reminded me of the teacher in the Charlie Brown cartoons—after a while her voice would just turn into gibberish in my head.

What really worked my nerves was how my mother never objected to what they said. After they left, when I would complain, my mother would say, "In Panama, every elder is considered the parent of the child. You could be walking down the street and if someone asked you to carry home a bag of groceries, you'd have to do it."

"Oh yeah, well, this isn't Panama," I'd say, giving her

my most evil look. "And if your friend isn't careful, I'm going to call Immigration on her."

"That isn't funny!" she would say, but I could see the smile on her face.

"Try me," I would say, mischievously. It was an idle threat, mostly because by this time, all of my mother's friends were citizens. But the thought of shipping those bossy women back to Panama, especially Esmerelda, was always a tantalizing daydream.

I wanted my mother to talk to me like she talked to these women. There was so much going on and because I didn't speak Spanish, I could only make out bits and pieces. I knew that besides the fact that he hardly ever showed up for his scheduled Saturday visits, my father had not paid one single child-support check and my mother had already taken him to court once. I wanted my mother to know that I was brave enough to hear her problems, courageous enough to face the severity that defined our day-to-day lives. That December, I heard my mother tell Esmerelda that she was only going to be able to spend a hundred dollars on presents for my brother and me. She'd have to spend the rest of her Christmas bonus on bills.

I sat down with the Sears Christmas catalogue. Every year my brother and I would flip through it in search of presents until the pages started to fall out. But this year, I decided to make a list of presents that totaled exactly fifty

dollars or less. This did not take a very long time. So I
made another list, then another, with different combina-
tions of presents.

- Barbie dolls (1 Barbie, 1 Ken) and a Holly Hobby
  Bake Set = $50.

  or
- One Christie (the black Barbie doll) plus a Barbie
  Corvette = $36

  or
- One Operation board game and the Holly Hobby
  Bake Set = $45

I must have come up with ten different combina-
tions. One night before I went to bed, I gave it to my
mother. She looked horrified. I was scared she was mad
at me. So often she was so quick and cruel in the way she
said no to our requests. "I will not beg, borrow, or steal
for you kids," she would say. "You'll make do with what
I can provide." But this evening, she held the list and just
looked down at the floor.

"What did I do wrong?" I asked.

"Nothing," she said quietly, kissing me good night.
"Go to bed."

The next day I told my brother to make a reasonable
list of presents within my mother's budget, but he refused, too young to see the gap between the hundred or

so presents he'd request and the three or four presents he'd receive. He knew my mother was Santa Claus, but he didn't think that it could also mean that she was poor. He knew what he wanted even if he wasn't going to get it. I envied his sense of entitlement, the way he always thought the world would unfold for him, no matter what. I had always reveled in being the "smarty pants" in the family, but this was a time when knowledge began to work against me. I had seen too many bad things and eavesdropped on too many of my mother's conversations ever to dream the way he was able to dream.

four

In my fifth-grade class, most of the boys were named Martin, Malcolm, Malik, or Muhammad. But the girls didn't have African names or names of great black leaders. Our names were meant to be pretty: Drena, Shannon, Teresa, Camille, Veronica. Throughout elementary school, before there was a Black History Month, there was a Black History Day. My mom and dad said that Malcolm and I could take the holiday only if we spent the day writing a report about a prominent black figure. These were our parents' rules, not the school's. I wrote about Martin Luther King and Shirley Chisolm and Rosa Parks. Every year, my brother wrote about Malcolm X, but my parents never seemed to mind.

Reading about black history, watching documentaries on t.v., it seemed that all the big black battles were over by the time I was born. My parents would talk about black people having to sit on the back of the bus and drink out of separate fountains, but that was so long ago. I loved to watch programs with Martin Luther King and Malcolm X giving speeches but the way I saw it, everybody who was black and important was also dead: Martin, Malcolm, Frederick Douglass, Harriet Tubman. All gone.

Watching footage of the bus boycotts, the sit-ins, and the marches on Channel 13, I would wonder if I would have been brave. My brother and I used to say, "No *way* were we sitting on the back of the bus!" but the look my mother would give us told me that we had no idea what we would have or wouldn't have done. Deep down inside, I wondered. As bad as those times were, I wished sometimes that there was some sort of protest or something important I could get involved with. In the black and white films about the movement, I would see girls my age with their hair pressed just so, wearing pretty white dresses and singing "We Shall Overcome." They looked like angels, and I wanted to be just like them.

In school we learned the Negro national anthem, "Lift Every Voice and Sing," which I tried to sing as sweetly and as loudly as I could even though my mother had already told me that I didn't have a singing voice. I read about people like Charlayne Hunter-Gault integrating colleges and I thought about my mother wanting to be a lawyer and not having the money to go to school and I felt like all that was changed now, there was no excuse for me not to be, as the old women in the neighborhood put it, "a credit to my race."

But my mother always warned me about aiming too high. "Don't always be pushing yourself ahead," she would say when I wanted to join something like the City Wide Band. I never understood how my mother could be so into the movement and at the same time, act as if we were just out of slavery days. It didn't make sense. If we had overcome, then why did it make her so nervous when I wanted to go out in the world and do things? It was almost like my mother had made two distinctions: one was a distinction between black people and white people, the other was the distinction between successful black people like Bill Cosby or Arthur Ashe and black people like us, who were poor and weren't on t.v.

"You can't do everything," she would say when I wanted to take acting lessons or dancing lessons. Which is why I was so surprised when my mother arranged for my brother to have private French lessons with her friend from Panama, Professor Alfred Rowe.

The first evening Professor Rowe came to our house, I could barely sit still, so I forced my mother to allow me to sit in on the lessons. I was planning on taking Spanish in junior high, and if I learned French on my own at home I would be trilingual just like my mother was. Professor Rowe gave my brother and me workbooks and began by teaching us pronouns and a few simple verbs. Two hours later when he said it was time to go, I couldn't believe it was over already.

Professor Rowe spent a few minutes in the kitchen with my mother while she paid him. As usual, I pretended to be busy conjugating verbs or something while I eavesdropped.

"I really appreciate this, Alfred," my mother said. "I know this is far less than your usual fee."

Professor Rowe laughed, in that deep charming way of his. "Come on, Cecilia. You and I go way back."

"I really think it will be good for Malcolm to have a man around once a week. He's really been acting up in school."

"He'll be fine," Professor Rowe said. "And Veronica is very bright. She picks up on things quickly."

I already understood that part of the logic of giving us French lessons was so that my brother could have yet another father figure. Finding male role models for my brother was all my mother thought about since the divorce. My father had married the woman he'd been having an affair with, and since she got pregnant, we hardly saw him at all anymore. My mother had begun to date again in the year since we'd moved to Ocean Avenue and while I liked the two or three men I had met, my mother made it clear that the person they were to impress was my brother.

"Maybe Anton could help you with your math homework?" my mother would say.

"Whatever," my brother would answer.

Then Anton would slip into dude mode and say, "Come on, Malcolm. Let's get your books, man. Let me see if I can help you out."

But none of the men my mother brought home could replace my father in my brother's eyes. He called my father constantly, begging him to pick us up for a visit. When my father would agree to a particular Saturday or Sunday, my brother would get up early that day, like it was Christmas, and get dressed and wait. I would get ready, too, but I was more skeptical. Sometimes my father would call hours after the appointed time to say he had "car trouble." Sometimes, he wouldn't call until days later. I refused to talk to him when he just didn't show up like that, but my brother was always more than happy to get on the phone.

One Saturday afternoon, my mother took my brother and me to the Avenue J flea market. The flea market was located in a big warehouse near the highway. It was sort of like a mall so you had to make sure you had your look straight when you went there because you always ran into someone from school. All the girls had Gheri curls—I did, too—and we would linger around the hair care products searching for the best goop to give our hair that "wet look." We would dress up in our Gloria Vanderbilt jeans and wear sweatshirts with our names appliquéd in felt letters. But it couldn't just be your name written plain—what you wrote on your sweatshirt had to have some style. Mine was a pink sweatshirt with black letters that spelled "Lady V." I thought it was cool, but not half as cool as LaTasha Jones's. The day I saw her at the flea market with a sweatshirt that said, "Keeping up with the Joneses," I almost died. She was so hip.

My mother always treated me and Malcolm to sour pickles from the pickle stand, and that's where we were when we ran into my father and my stepmother. My stepmother's stomach was so big she looked like she was going to drop a baby any minute. My father and stepmother both acted as if we were all good friends, smiling and saying, "Hi!" My brother dropped his bags and gave my father a bear hug and then turned around and hugged my stepmother as well. I looked up at my mother, searching for the pain that might not show on her face. My father gestured for me to hug him, but I didn't move from my mother's side. We all just stood there for a while staring at each other, trying to carry on like we all didn't hate each other. After a couple of seconds, my mother said, "Come on, Malcolm, it's time to go."

"No, I want to stay with Daddy," my brother said,

giving my mother a defiant look like somehow she was the bad guy.

I expected her to smack him, but she didn't say a word. Instead my father pushed my brother toward us and said, "We've got a lot of errands to run. But I'll catch up with you on Saturday, little man."

The whole way home, my mother walked in silence. She didn't say a word when I tried to hold her hand, she wouldn't grasp it. She was like a rag doll, her arms hanging limply at her sides.

After my father had blown off several visits in a row, I decided I wasn't going to put up with it anymore. One day after school, I told my father that I didn't want to speak to him ever again. He was furious.

"I'm your father. Goddamnit. You don't fuck with me," he said, screaming into the phone. "I'm going to come to your school tomorrow and beat your ass for being so rude to me."

That night when my mother came home from work I told her what my father had said. I told her I was afraid to go to school tomorrow because my father might be waiting for me.

"Put your shoes on," my mother said. "We're going for a walk."

She left my brother with Flora and the two of us went downstairs to the street. We walked for more than an hour until I was in a part of Brooklyn that I didn't recognize. I chattered along about school and my friends, but my mother didn't answer with more than a nod and an "Uh-huh." Finally I recognized the block where my stepmother lived, where my father had been living since he'd left us.

"I'm scared, Mommy," I said. I was hungry, too.

"There's nothing to be scared of," she said.

She approached the building and rang my step-mother's doorbell. My father answered the buzzer and when he heard it was my mother, he said he would come downstairs. Seconds later, he materialized, dressed as usual in his three-piece suit, ready to go on stage.

"What's going on?" he said, ignoring me.

"Did you threaten my child?" my mother asked him, calmly.

"What are you talking about? She won't talk to me on the phone, she's disrespecting me!" my father said.

"She won't talk to you because you never show up when you say you will. She's mad at you and she has a right. But she has to respect you because you're her fa-ther." Then she turned to me. "Do you hear me? I won't have you disrespecting your father. Don't raise your voice at him. Don't hang up the phone on him. Don't curse at him."

I nodded, staring at the square of concrete beneath me, grateful that he hadn't knocked me to the ground.

"But you don't go around threatening her, you hear

me?" my mother said. "I'll punish her if she does wrong. But don't you scare her because nobody's going to beat her ass but me. Good night."

Then she turned around, took my hand, and we walked home. I knew then just how strong the divorce had made my mother. Even though there had been times when she could not protect herself, my mother was going to protect me. So many times when my father had hit my mother, I'd felt helpless. I worried that because I was a girl, because I wasn't physically strong, I'd have to put up with the same sorts of things when I was a grown-up. Watching my mother put my father in check, I knew then that it wasn't about being a girl, it wasn't about how tall or muscular you were. Strong was strong. And it had to be built up on the inside.

After the divorce, I began to see how my mother's life could have been different without my father, without us even. "I wanted to be a lawyer," she had told me. "But there was no money for that." Her choices were sewing school or secretarial school; she chose secretarial school. I knew that I was a product of my mother's lack of choice.

One day my mom was talking on the phone to a friend and she joked, "If abortion had been legal . . ." She said it in a mischievous and giddy tone she rarely used, but still it sent me into a panic.

I slid away from the kitchen door and tried to figure out if I had heard her right. When she slipped back and forth between English and Spanish, I wasn't always so sure. But I knew I had heard her correctly. If my brother had been home, I could have picked on him. But he was at our cousins', so I decided to go to my room and sulk.

∿

I lie on my bed with my arms at my sides. This is where I come to freak out. I hold my hands in fists, squeezing until my nails dig into my flesh. Then I stare at the ceiling until I have studied every corner. Ceilings are hard to know because we spend so little time looking up, but if I close my eyes I can picture this ceiling just like I can imagine a picture hanging on the wall. When my body feels useless, the ceiling is where I go. I stare and stare until I can imagine myself walking on the ceiling and the ceiling is the floor and the floor is the ceiling. I sit on the ceiling.

My mother worries me. I know I am not a grown-up, but I know what I see. Taking care of us is wearing my poor mommy to the bone. She is like a ship sinking under her own weight and I want to help. I feel like tossing things over the side, anything to keep her afloat. If she could do it, if she could stop the sinking, what would she toss? Me? My brother? I want her to stand straight, not slumped. I want to see her laugh and play. She is only thirty, younger and prettier than all my friends' mothers. I want to see her laughing. I want to see her sailing in the wind.

I get out of bed and I tear a piece of paper out of my notebook. I get a pen and I start to play the age game. My mother does not know I play it, but I play it all the time. My mother was twenty years old when she had me, so I always know exactly how old she is because all I have to do is add twenty to my age. I make two columns like this:

ME	MOMMY
10	30
20	40
30	50
40	60
50	70
60	80
70	90
80	100

I figure that when I am eighty, maybe then I'll be able to deal with her dying and leaving me. So in my mind, I will her to live to a hundred, or ninety at least.

My grandma Flora is in her eighties and I try not to think about her dying. She tells me that there are things I must learn because I am getting to be a big girl—how to wash the dishes without breaking a glass every time, how to make a bed with flat sheets, not just fitted ones, how to iron a man's shirt.

I think it's strange that Flora wants to teach me how to iron a man's shirt because there are no men in our house. But Flora worked all her life in the laundry in the Canal Zone, ironing shirts for the American soldiers. She says ironing shirts helped her feed seven children and put my mother through secretarial school and that's why she's able to take care of us today.

Where the man's shirt came from, I don't know. Maybe it was one of my father's that got moved with our stuff when we left Beverly Road. Maybe it was one of my uncles' that Flora brought back after visiting there for a weekend. It hangs on the ironing board, white and lifeless. Flora tells me to plug in the iron and to get the starch and a cup of water. So I do.

"How do you know if the iron is hot?" she asks me.

I touch the iron and burn myself. "It's hot," I say.

She puts her hand in the cup of water and splashes a few drops on the face of the iron. I watch them sizzle. "This way is better," she says.

She tells me to hold the iron and I tremble with the weight of it in my hand. I keep thinking it will jump away from me and burn my arms and legs. Flora stands behind me and over my shoulder positions the shirt so that the back panel lies flat.

"You iron this part first," she says. My hand wobbles

as I move the iron and she covers my hand with hers and I jump a little. For all the wrinkles she has on top of her hand, her palm is smooth and cool like a piece of brown silk.

She stands behind me ironing and I inhale her smell— a mixture of medicine, Ben-Gay, Jergens lotion, and perfumed powder. I try to pay attention as she shows me how to starch the collar and iron in between buttonholes, but I keep losing myself in her smell. She shows me how to iron pants next and turns the pants inside out, ironing the pockets flat before ironing the creases into the pants. I ask her, "Why do we have to iron the pockets when nobody's going to see them?"

"*Las cosas se hacen bien o no se hacen,*" she says. Do things well or don't do things at all. It is a typical response, something my mother says again and again. But I don't get it. Especially because it seems to apply only to housework, which I am bad at, not schoolwork, which I am good at.

∾

Flora was already eighty-three when she went into the hospital with water in the lungs. She always took pills for arthritis and a heart condition, but this was more serious. My mother was scared, she felt like she couldn't watch her die. She called a friend from Panama and went to

Boston for the weekend. That weekend, Flora died. She had only been in the hospital for three days.

At the funeral, my aunt Diana and my cousins were sobbing hysterically. But my mother was dry-eyed, so I didn't cry either. My uncle tugged my shoulder as I walked up to the coffin. "You're a tough girl like your mother," he whispered. "That woman raised her and not a tear in her eye." But I knew that wasn't why my mother hadn't cried. I'd heard her talking on the phone to her friend in Boston.

"I'm totally alone now," my mother had said, her voice tiny like a baby's. "I'm totally alone." I heard her talking about how much the funeral cost and how my father had cleaned out her savings account before the divorce. She had to borrow money to "bury Flora right." I think she was too scared to let herself cry.

They told me that at the hospital, before she died, Flora had asked for me and that meant she was thinking of me as she passed away and that she would always protect me. I comforted myself in this, and when I was alone or afraid, I felt as if I could feel her standing behind me like the day she taught me to iron.

The next year, when I began junior high school, I got a job ironing shirts for a bachelor who lived in our building. I made twenty-five cents a shirt and twenty-five cents for a pair of pants. I could make three or four dollars a week ironing, a few bucks more if I walked his dog after school. It wasn't a ton of money, but I could go to the early movie when it was half price and I always had quarters if I wanted to buy a chocolate bar.

After Flora died, my mother decided that my brother and I could not spend the summers alone, unsupervised. "It's too easy to get in trouble, with all that time on your hands," she said. The first summer she sent us to day camp. I went to Girl Scout camp. My brother went to day camp at the local YMCA. I knew it was a sacrifice for her, but day camp was disappointing. It was like one long recess and the next thing you knew you were back on the bus, on your way home again. I wanted to go to sleep-away camp, not for the whole summer, but just for August. I always imagined August would be the perfect time to go to the woods—since it was close to September, I saw August as being just a little cooler than July. I thought August was a good month to learn how to canoe, make s'mores, sleep in a tent—all the stuff I'd seen kids on t.v. do. Common sense could have told me that August was no cooler than July; every summer I felt the heat just like everybody else. But I liked the word August, the way it rolled off my tongue, so like ice cream. I thought that August would be smooth and creamy and cool.

The summer I was eleven, my mother arranged for

me to spend July and August "down south" with her friend's parents. Her friend had been our neighbor on Beverly Road and her daughter Jayne and I had played together though we didn't really get along. On Beverly Road, there had never been any question about who were the black girls from the islands and who were the black girls from America. In the summer, right after the last day of school, our black American girlfriends would be shipped down south until Labor Day. The rest of us, whose families came from so far away—places you couldn't drive to and we couldn't afford to fly to—would walk down the street feeling abandoned and lonely.

The black history books my parents gave me made me think that the South was the scariest place you could ever be. But my friends would get all excited and talk about the fried chicken their grandmothers would make, the bikes they would ride down there, the cute boys they would meet. I didn't know how to ride a bike. My mother didn't know how so she couldn't teach me. Besides, she said, it was too dangerous in the city. We never, ever had fried chicken in my house. My mother didn't know how to make it. The only fried chicken we ate was the occasional bucket from KFC. I envied these girls, their extended families only a bus ride away. I missed the girls that I was tight with. We girls from the islands would make temporary alliances, choose temporary best friends and temporary hang-out spots until the other girls got back to the city and things were normal again. But this summer was going to be different, this summer I was going down south, too.

My mother didn't seem afraid for me. She said we were lucky that Jayne's grandparents were nice enough to take me in. She said I had to try to budget the money she gave me and she would send more when she could. She told me to behave myself and not to ask for anything I wasn't given.

My brother was supposed to spend the summer with my father. My mother was furious when she found out that my father was sending him to Guyana to spend the summer with my stepmother's family. When my brother came back that September, he moved in with my father and stepmother permanently.

My friendship with Jayne, shaky to begin with, deteriorated into nothing in Florida. She was her grandparents' favorite and although they were kind, I felt out of place. Luckily, there was a girl who lived across the street named Fredericka who adopted me as her summer best friend. I know because she told me so. And I remember thinking for the first time that maybe my girlfriends who went down south were lonely, too.

Fredericka lived in a house that was four times the size of Jayne's grandparents'. It had a sunroom with really nice furniture and a beautiful wood ceiling fan with brass trimmings. I loved going over to Freddie's house because the minute you stepped through the door it felt like walking through the gates of heaven. It was that cool. Sometimes I would come in, then go out again, just so I could come in again. Freddie's mother would simply not have it. She'd say, "Girl, you better stop opening and closing my door before I leave you out there to roast."

I wrote my mother about Freddie, making a point of talking about Jayne and her grandparents as little as possible. She called once or twice, but I didn't call her because it was so expensive. All summer I had so much fun, I didn't really miss my mother. At the airport, she had let me know that she wouldn't be missing me and my brother much either. "Are you going to be bored?" I'd asked her, feeling sorry for her.

"Bored?" she said, laughing. "I'm going to enjoy the peace and quiet."

When I came back from Florida, it was just my mother and me. I thought when my brother moved in with my father, my mother and I would get closer. But it was like my brother's leaving made us less of a family. Alone, my mother and I were like roommates who tried to stay out of each other's way. So many times, I had been jealous of the attention my mother gave my brother and I hated sharing her with him. But with my brother out of the picture, I didn't feel like an only child. My mother was still worried about him, she still bought him school clothes when she bought clothes for me. If anything, the sadness my mother felt about my brother's leaving made her serious and unhappy, like she had been before the divorce. I had hoped my mother would talk to me, treat me like her girlfriend, but if anything, she kept more things to herself.

ᕽ

My new best friend in the seventh grade was a girl named Ileana. Ileana and her mother attended the local Lutheran church. They would always invite me and my mother to attend services, but my mother always declined, though she would tell me that I could go. She would get up, help me get dressed, and then go back to sleep. When I came home in the afternoon, she'd be dressed in her home clothes and cooking Sunday dinner.

I began attending church regularly with Ileana. I joined her confirmation class and was confirmed that spring. One day, I came home from church early and I saw my mother coming out of the Catholic church down the block. She was walking ahead of me, dressed in a nice shirt and pants, and I was surprised because when I left for church that morning, she was sleeping. I ran to catch up with her and I grabbed her sleeve. She didn't look half as shocked as I was. In fact, she didn't look surprised at all.

"How long have you been a Catholic?" I asked her.

"All my life," she said.

"How often do you go to that church?"

"Whenever I feel like it."

The tone in her voice told me not to ask any more questions. Her religion was her affair. And if I wanted to attend the Lutheran church with Ileana it was mine to do.

 ∾

When I became interested in boys and boys became interested in me, I did not discuss any of it with my mother. She told me that I could not go out on dates. I took that to mean evening dates, alone with boys. I figured that after-school dates, with boys and girls, didn't count so I didn't ask permission and I tried not to get in trouble. When I got my period, my mother handed me a box of Kotex and made me a cup of tea. She wasn't cold about it, but she made it clear that it was no big deal. When I was eight years old, she'd asked me if I knew where babies came from. I'd told her yes, I'd read about it in a book. That was the last conversation we had on the topic.

As I entered my teens, my mother never warned me not to have sex. She never told me not to get pregnant. She asked me if I knew about birth control and I told her yes. Again, end of discussion. I knew that my aunt had gotten pregnant as a teenager. And that my mother, feeling that disgrace had come twice to the family when she

got pregnant, married my father, a man she did not love.
Yet my mother never told me what not to do, as if the
very act of forbidding it would make her worst expecta-
tions come true. Her nonchalance about the matter of
my sexuality made me think that she was bracing herself
for the inevitable.

But I'd already decided that I could prevent what was
the norm in my neighborhood by not sleeping with anybody at all. I had seen girls talk about how their men
loved them, only to have the guys ditch them when the
girls became pregnant. Most of our mothers were single
and by ninth grade, all of my friends who had babies were
single mothers, too. So no matter how much a boy said
that he loved me, that he'd be careful, that he had rubbers,
that he knew how to do it so it wouldn't hurt and I
wouldn't get pregnant, I always said no. No guy ever said
a word to me that didn't sound like a lie. There was never
a time when I thought, "Well, maybe. Just this time." The
answer was always no. As my friend Howard used to say, I
was on serious lockdown. Like Sing Sing or Alcatraz.

I had this dream of going to college and I couldn't let
it go. My teachers told me that I was smart, that I could
get scholarships. In the library, I read through college
guides and along with Harvard, I added other names
to the list of my dream colleges: NYU, Bryn Mawr,
Howard, and Spelman. I would tell my mother about
these colleges and she would nod, uninterested. It was

like when she wouldn't promise me an allowance because she didn't want me to be mad at her if she couldn't come through. College was my dream, my house of cards to build. If it might not work out, she wasn't going to have any part of it.

My mother always made it clear that happiness wasn't something you could expect out of life. "All I have to do is pay taxes and die," she would say, and I hated the way she sounded like those black women in church, talking about getting their piece of the pie in heaven. My mother let it be known that I couldn't walk around expecting the world to make me happy. She was the one working hard to pay the bills and she wasn't about to tolerate my moodiness.

All my life I'd gotten the message that black women were strong and that black women do *not* get depressed. It was a falsehood, of course, like the other myths that said that black women do not have eating disorders or go to therapy. But it remained throughout my childhood a popular falsehood that demarcated depression as white girls' domain.

These myths were corroborated by everything and everyone around me. In church on Sunday, I saw women dressed impeccably, singing and swinging and getting merry like Christmas. Maybe some of these women were depressed, maybe they secretly hated their bodies. I wondered this as I watched the big black women with breasts that could smother a child and the rail-thin women whose very existence seemed to hiss, "I may be old, I may be black. But I'll be *damned* if I'll be old, black, and fat." What does thinness mean, what price are you willing to pay, when in your nightmares there are a thousand Mammys and all of them have your face? But nobody spoke of the pain, and on Sunday, the women were all smiles in their brightly colored dresses and elaborately plumed hats. The message in church was clear: lay your burdens and your secrets down by the riverside.

At the hair salon, I would catch snippets of conversation about women who weren't feeling so good about life. Their depression (though that word was never used) was proved by the fact that they hadn't been to the salon lately. These women were "sick" because they were "letting themselves go." The beauticians always knew whose man had left, who'd been laid off from her job, and who had the blues. Not having money was not excuse enough not to have your hair done. I watched women hand the hairdresser a five-dollar bill for a fifteen-dollar perm, and whisper, "I'll catch up when I get paid next week." When the women didn't show up at all, they left themselves open to all sorts of criticism. "Not doing her hair or her nails, child," I would hear the hairdresser say as she tugged the straightening comb through my hair. "Saw her the other day at Pathmark. Chipped red nail polish . . . and you know how bad red looks when it's chipped." But these sad women were rarely seen; in their depressed states, they hid out like emotionally disfigured lepers in their colony.

In my own family, there was often chat about my "crazy Aunt Gena." I knew Aunt Gena and I liked her because she wore glasses, a symbol to me of her intelligence and the college degree that was so rare in our family. Gena also had a sexy, deep voice and as a single "career girl" she reminded me of a black Lauren Bacall. Everything about her seemed worth emulating.

Best of all, Gena never showed up at our house empty-handed. She would always bring me and my brother presents—late birthday presents and late Christmas presents wrapped in Santa Claus paper in the heat of July. There was an ad on t.v. for Crazy Eddie, a home electronics store, in which the guy in the commercial would scream, "Christmas sales in July! *It's insane!*" But that was my aunt Gena in real life. Looking at the Santa Claus paper, I would wonder if the gift had been sitting in her house since Christmas or if she had purposely chosen the wrapping paper. It was hard to tell.

Like the women discussed in the salon, Aunt Gena would also disappear from time to time. I would hear older relatives talking about going up to her house in the Bronx and finding her unshowered and locked in her bedroom, a month's worth of garbage piled in the kitchen. The thought scared me. "*What* is wrong with her?" I would ask, only to be hushed and sent away by my mother and a cadre of aunts and cousins.

I mentioned feeling depressed myself only one time to my mother. I was thirteen years old. It was a Sunday afternoon and my mother and I had both returned home from our respective churches. My mother had changed into her house clothes and dinner was cooking in the kitchen. She was standing at the glass étagère in our living room. She had been taping a salsa program off the local radio station and had come from the kitchen to flip the tape. I walked up to her and said, "Mom, I'm really depressed." The gale force with which she spun around could have knocked over a four-hundred-pound man.

"What do *you* have to be depressed about?" She demanded an answer, and the tone in her voice told me it better be good. I didn't say anything. "I bust my ass forty hours a week to put a roof over your head, clothes on your back, food on your table, and you're *depressed*?" All of a sudden the fact that the cutest guy in school didn't notice me and I was about to fail math again and my best friend had abandoned me for a cooler posse seemed pretty meaningless.

I remember seeing a magic act when I was little in which the magician would repeat over and over: "The closer you get, the less you can see." And oddly enough, it was true. The people in the front row couldn't see through the deception; they were so close, yet they were looking for the wrong thing while the trick was being pulled right before their eyes. Black women are masters of emotional sleight of hand. The closer you get, the less you can see. It was true of my mother. It is also true of me.

five

In New York City, when you're in the eighth grade, you can apply to any number of specialized high schools. There's Brooklyn Technical and Bronx High School of Science, the Clara Barton School for Nursing and the High School of the Performing Arts, which was forever memorialized in the movie *Fame*.

When I was thirteen, I got the booklet listing all the high schools and their specialties. I was excited about being able to go to a specialized school though I couldn't really interest my friends in it. The brainiest kids would be going to one of the high schools that emphasized math and science like Brooklyn Tech or Bronx Science. Math and science were my worst subjects. Most of my friends would be going to the high school in our zoning region, but I didn't want to go there because it had a reputation for being a place where girls got jumped.

The older I got, the more fighting I had to do. As much as I loved school, being there got rougher and rougher. Usually if a girl was trying to boss you around, she would just get in your face. I'd been slapped and knocked down a couple of times. If you didn't fight back, usually it wouldn't go too far. But having been hit by my father made me jumpy, easy to scare. The girls who would pick on me reminded me of my father because their outbursts were just as unpredictable. You could be totally cool with a girl one afternoon, then the next day when you walked into the homeroom, she would be all over you. "Tamika said that you were talking about me last week," or "I'm sick and tired of your bull-shit two-facedness." I used to try to get to the bottom of the matter—tracking down Tamika, talking to other girls to get them to be on my side—but I soon gave that up. There was no bottom of the matter. It wasn't about right or wrong. It was about somebody wanting to kick some ass and your name working its way to the top of the list.

I never talked to my mother about the fights I would get into. But one weekend I had a fight with a girl named Kara and there was no way I could hide it. Kara and I had been best friends. Over the summer, I'd begun to "go with" a guy named Trevor who was in high school, a few years older than us, a big catch. "Ooo, he's fine," Kara would say when Trevor would stop by after school. "And you don't have to give up the skins, either?" she would say, in reference to the fact that even though I was dating an older guy, I wasn't sleeping with him.

One Saturday afternoon, Trevor came over to see me and Kara was in full flirt mode. "Baby, you know you look good, right?" she said. Kara was tall and shapely, with a short Afro that framed her ebony face perfectly. She was pretty and was used to getting her way.

Trevor kind of grinned. "So how you doing, Kara?" he said. Kara continued flirting with Trevor until I felt uncomfortable enough to say something.

"Okay, quit it, Kara," I said, with a tight little laugh in my voice. Trevor and I were sitting on the steps of my building. Kara was leaning over the railing, trying to give Trevor a good look at her cleavage.

Kara turned and looked at me as if I were a total stranger. "What did you say, bitch?"

"I said cool it. Okay, Kara?"

"No, it's not okay," she said. Before I knew it, she'd punched me in the face and I was down on the floor. Besides the fact that I was a complete wimp, I knew I could never hit someone the way I'd been hit. I'd rather just take it without fighting back, I thought, convincing myself that this was the moral high ground. As I tried to block Kara's punches, I kept thinking that Trevor or somebody would jump in and break it up. But Trevor was nowhere to be found and the worst had happened, a small crowd had gathered around us and they were cheering Kara on.

"Kick her ass, Kara. Stomp her! Like that." The West Indian kids shouting, "*Buyaka!*"

Next thing I knew I was being dragged away and onto the elevator by my mother's friend Esmerelda. I knew there'd be hell to pay on Monday. It was one thing to get your ass kicked. It was another thing entirely to have your mother's friend break it up. In the meantime, I was just grateful for the reprieve. My mother put ice on my face while Esmerelda told her what happened. I was crying softly to myself, never so glad to have my mommy, when she looked down at me with a chilling gaze.

"I heard you were just lying there," my mother said, examining my head.

"I was trying not to fight, I just was trying to protect myself," I said.

"Look, I can't be here every day with you," she said. "If I'm going to have to worry about you getting beat up, then you're going to have to stay inside until I come home from work."

"What?" I said. "I can't do that! That's not fair!"

She looked at me hard. "Then next time, fight back."

I was shocked. I expected sympathy. She expected me to stand up for myself. So I couldn't come running to my mother when people hurt me. I didn't get into many fights after that, but the few I did, I kept to myself.

I would begin high school that fall. The local high school would be a free-for-all, and I knew I didn't want to go there. If I went to a specialized high school, I could concentrate more on school and less on saving my ass. But when I brought the booklet home to my mother, she told me, "Choose whatever interests you," while she poured too much pepper sauce into the *arroz con pollo.*

"Well, what do *you* think sounds interesting?" I said, dragging one of the dining room chairs into the kitchen. "Which one would you choose?"

"I'm not choosing, you are," she said. She wasn't going to give a single inch.

"I'm thinking about Murray Bergtraum, that's the school for business careers. Or Fashion Industries, that's for fashion design and merchandising."

"That sounds good," she said, never turning her attention away from the food.

My mother seemed to prize the way that Grandma Flora had given her the choice, when she was about my age, between sewing school and secretarial school. But I wanted to tell her that I wasn't like her. I wanted someone to tell me what to do. But I never did. My mother had a way of shutting down and as pushy as I was, when she drew the line, I was never brave enough to cross it.

I was wait-listed at Murray Bergtraum and accepted at

Fashion Industries. I decided to "major" in fashion merchandising while taking college prep classes. I liked Fashion High, although the scene in the cafeteria was so rough that a girl named Alexandra and I took to eating our lunch in the twelfth-floor stairwell just to avoid all the people popping shit. Every year, the design students designed clothing and put on a fashion show that the merchandising students ran. There was also a little boutique that sold jewelry and scarves and stockings, so if you ripped your hose in third period, you could run down and get another pair.

That Thanksgiving, my mother went to visit her brother in California. When she came back, she announced that she'd met a man, a man she had known in Panama, and that we were moving to Los Angeles to live with him by Christmas. I couldn't believe it. I couldn't believe that she was making me move somewhere I'd never been, to live with a man I'd never met. Before, she'd brought her boyfriends by the apartment, and while my brother and I never had the right to veto them, we definitely could voice an opinion. Now we were moving to Los Angeles and I had no say whatsoever.

My mother went out there first to find an apartment and get things ready. I stayed with my aunt Diana to finish out the semester. My aunt laughed when she talked about my mother. "She's always been a gypsy, always been pigheaded. When she's got something in her head, that's it." My cousin Guille wondered what my stepfather would be like and I did, too.

My brother had been having a string of fights with my stepmother, which resulted in him staying with various aunts "until things cooled off." After two months, it was clear the situation was permanent. My aunt Amelia's oldest son, Robert, was my brother's best friend, so Malcolm loved living over there. I called my brother after school one day to talk about the move to California.

"Do you think you'd want to come with us?" I ventured. In the face of moving in with a stepfather I'd never met, it suddenly occurred to me that my previously pesky brother could be an ally.

"Mommy didn't invite me to go," he said stubbornly. "Besides, I'm in school with Robert. I don't want to change schools now."

"But California is really sunny, all those beaches and stuff," I said, sounding like a tourism campaign.

"Mommy didn't invite me," my brother said again, and I could feel the sting in his voice.

"Just tell her you want to come. You're the one who wanted to move in with Daddy, so you should ask to come back."

"Forget it, V," he said.

"Well," I said, disappointed. "You better come visit."

In spite of myself, I grew more and more excited about the move. By the ninth grade I would have already attended seven schools. I had begun to look at each new school as a chance to reinvent myself, to decide whether I wanted to be called Veronica or Victoria or Vicki, to try out new hairstyles and new after-school activities. After my mother left in early December, I spent the next few weeks saying good-bye to my friends and dreaming about the new place. I was nervous about my stepfather, but I figured I'd deal with him when I got there.

At the airport in New York, my aunt Diana gave me my Christmas present. It was a beautiful makeup kit with eyeshadows, lipsticks, blush, and a little mirror. I loved it so much, I felt like my aunt was acknowledging that I was really grown up. When the plane landed in L.A., I hurried to put it on so that my mother could see my new look.

I could tell something was wrong when my mother met me at the gate. She kissed me on the cheek, but she didn't seem at all thrilled to see me. She didn't notice all the makeup I'd piled onto my face. My stepfather, Tono, was not what I had expected at all—he was stiff and serious. The whole ride home nobody spoke. Nobody asked me how the flight was, nobody said, "Welcome to California!" I had that feeling I used to get as a little kid— that I was in trouble but I didn't know why. I'd just arrived. What could I have done?

"Where's our tree?" I asked my mother when we got back to our apartment.

She ignored the question and went into the kitchen. "Are you hungry?" she asked.

"Yes, I'm hungry. But where's the Christmas tree?"

My mother sat down, a weary look on her face. "The job I had lined up didn't work out. I'm looking for work. Tono is looking for work. We've got to make our money last."

I heard the words coming out of her mouth but I couldn't believe what she was saying. My mother *lived* for Christmas. She started decorating the tree on the first of December and didn't take it down until January 3. No matter how broke we were, we'd never gone without a tree.

"Well, here are your presents," I said, taking two giftwrapped items out of my bag. "Where are mine?"

"There aren't any presents for you, V," my mother said, stirring some food on the stove.

"You don't have a credit card now either?"

My stepfather piped in and I was startled by his voice. "Veronica," he said. "That's enough."

"Where is my room?" I asked. It was time to do some serious thinking. I'd only met this man a few hours ago and already he was butting into our business. Who did he think he was?

My mother gave me no presents that Christmas or any after that. Even when she was working again, she'd say, "Presents are for kids," or "Christmas is too materialistic. I'm giving money to charities instead." She stopped giving me birthday presents, too. It was like she'd decided she'd already given me enough and didn't need to give me another thing ever again.

∾

My stepfather and I never warmed to each other. Having spent his entire adulthood in the military, he expected our house to be run much the same way. The more he tried to correct me, to teach me the formalities he was used to, the more I couldn't stand him. After a while, he stopped addressing me altogether. He would say something in Spanish to my mother and then she would turn around and order me to do it. I'd begun to study Spanish in school and could speak and understand it well. But the minute I objected to him, he would proceed with this ridiculous chain of command. My mother wasn't voicing her ideas, she was only repeating what he told her to say.

I hated Los Angeles. Our palm tree–lined street, which had seemed so beautiful on my first day, was right in the heart of Crips territory. I found this out the first day I wore red to school. A tall girl with three scars on her face walked up to me in front of our apartment building after school.

"What set you from?" she asked accusingly.

"What?"

"Don't fuck with me, bitch," she said, and I prepared for a beat down, New York style.

Luckily I'd become friends with a girl named Linda who could really fight. Linda went up to the girl and said, "Yo, she don't gang-bang. She's from New York."

"Oh yeah?" the girl said, looking me up and down. "Well, she better act like she know."

I told my mother that I couldn't wear red to school—unfortunate because a lot of my clothes were red. My mother liked me to wear bright colors. She told me not to be ridiculous, that I couldn't let other kids tell me what to wear. But the first time she heard the Crips go through our neighborhood blasting their guns just to make people jump, she realized how serious it was.

L.A. was a nightmare. I didn't get along with my stepfather. I was afraid to hang out on the street. The guy gang members were bad, but the girls would scratch your eyes out just for looking at them funny. At night, when I did my homework, I could hear gunshots from blocks away. As rough as our block in Brooklyn had been, guns were still not an everyday thing.

The local school was on a year-round system and when my mother took me to be registered, I was told that I would join "the green track." I asked the counselor if this was "the gifted and talented program" and she just stared at me. My mother looked uncomfortable because she knew that I was getting ready to "push myself ahead."

The counselor coughed, then mumbled, "No. That is the blue track and they're on vacation until February." I told her that I needed to be in the accelerated program and looked to my mother for support, but my mother said nothing. I knew that by myself, asking to be in "gifted and talented" made me sound like a whiny brat. If my mother insisted on it, too, the school was more likely to pay attention. The counselor looked at my mother for a moment, absorbed her silence, and I knew I was sunk.

"Why don't we do this?" she said. "Green track starts on Monday and you can begin with them. If you get all A's in everything, then next year, we'll arrange for you to be on blue track."

"This is the last year!" I was furious. "There is no next year! Next year, we'll be in high school."

The counselor just smiled at me. "Well, let's see how you do."

I had no choice. I started green track and as I expected, the work was too easy and the kids were kind of tough. In February, when the blue-track kids came back, what had been a barely tolerable situation became pure agony. The blue-track kids were golden—they were the most popular, adored by the teachers, soloists in sports and theater and the band. At other schools, the accelerated program had been special but nerdy. At this school, the blue-track kids got everything.

Every day, I felt like I was crawling deeper into a

hole. I wanted to be with them. I felt like I belonged with them, but even though I was sleep-walking through my classes and all my teachers said I was way ahead, my counselor wouldn't approve the transfer. I knew that I'd pushed too far and my attitude had turned her off. She was never going to help me.

I learned that the principal at the school had an arrangement with Choate Rosemary Hall, a boarding school back East. Every year, Choate offered a full three-year scholarship to one black student from South Central. Every year, it was an intense competition as the handful of kids selected to apply began their weeks-long fantasy about getting this scholarship and getting the hell out of the hood. One by one, students were called to the principal's office for a meeting in which they were handed the application. By March, when the applications were all handed out, I'd become friends with some of the blue-track students. It took me a week to figure out that the only students invited to apply were blue-track students. I wasn't even going to get a chance.

My mother didn't have a clue as to what this meant to me. She was always trying to get me to slow down, but when I heard about places like Choate, when I thought about colleges like Harvard, I knew there was no way I could slow down. One day, I was going to make it out of these bad neighborhoods and these piss-poor schools where I had to beg for real work. I knew my mother wasn't going to help me, even if I didn't know why. But if I could make it, then I hoped and prayed she would see I'd done the right thing and one day she would be proud.

Every day at lunch, Jamie, one of the football stars on blue track, would talk about going to Choate Rosemary. He even took to wearing pastel cardigans with the Izod Lacoste insignia "for luck." He would tell anyone who would listen, "You know it's going to be me. This scholarship is all about me." The thing is, it wasn't like applying to colleges, there wasn't a wide selection of Choate Rosemarys to apply to. There was only one scholarship and you couldn't reapply if you blew it because it was only given once a year to the most promising ninth-grader.

Like black Cinderellas, every bright kid tried on the glass slipper, except the shoe never even came my way. Every night, I prayed that the principal would call me. A week before the applications were due, I grew desperate. I summoned the courage to go and see him. I knocked on the principal's door and asked him if I could apply for the scholarship. "Oh, but of course. Of course," he said, and picked up the phone as he motioned for me to sit down. "Hello, Bob," he said in a deep rolling voice that made me think of great black orators like Frederick Douglass. "Can you send along another application, there's a tenacious young lady here who is perfectly capable but was somehow overlooked. Okay, thank you, Bob."

I filled out the Choate application with so much anticipation. In the excruciating weeks that followed, I thumbed the catalogue until the pages started to come loose from the binding. My mother reacted to all this like it was bad news. I read once that Zora Neale Hurston's mother had told her, "Jump at de sun, chile. You may not reach it, but at least you'll get off the ground." I didn't understand my mother at all; what had happened since the days of the movement? Wasn't this the point of it all—to give black boys and girls like me a chance to fly?

"I don't understand this thing about going away to high school," my mother said. I sat in the living room with all the Choate material on my lap. My mother wouldn't even glance at the catalogue. She kept her hand on the remote and her eyes on the television.

"It's boarding school, like *The Facts of Life,*" I said, trying not to sound too rude or angry. *The Facts of Life* used to be my favorite show. When I heard about Choate, I instantly thought about how I used to dream of being Tootie, the cute roller-skating black student on the show.

"You want to go away to college and now you want to go away to high school, I don't understand this."

What I wanted to say was this: *Go away? Of course I'm going away! The sooner, the better. What part don't you understand?* Those grades that she had no time for would get me a scholarship to college. College would mean a better life. Of course I was going away. Didn't she want me to have a better life?

What I said was, "Just look at the brochure." I moved closer to her, showing her the pages as if it was a picture book, as if I were the mother reading to my child. "It's a really beautiful campus with really good teachers. I could take much better classes than I could take at any school around here."

My mother refused to look. "You're going to do what you want to do."

I felt so many different things at once: angry at my mother for refusing to pay attention to my dreams; suspicious that deep down she wanted me to go away to school so that she could be alone with my stepfather. He was always muttering to her in Spanish these days and more and more she was on my back about how I dressed, what time I came in, doing chores. It was never like that when it was just the two of us. Plus, I was scared of the neighborhood. I needed Choate Rosemary more than I ever needed anything before. I went through the course catalogue deciding what languages I would study (Spanish and Russian) and what sport I would play (tennis). Since Connecticut was close to New York, I thought I could stay with my grandmother on my father's side during vacations. As much as Jamie talked about Choate being his destiny, it had to be mine.

But when the time came, neither of us got the scholarship. It went instead to a quiet, intensely brilliant Nigerian girl. I felt like I was in mourning for days. I stared at the girl from across the lunchroom. I watched the simple way she dressed, how softly she spoke, the way she read quietly while the rest of us goofed around. I was smart, but I wasn't smart enough. The next time, I thought, I'll try harder. I'll spend more time on my essays, I'll start reading more books. The next time, whenever and whatever it was, it would be my turn. One day, it would *have* to be my turn.

At the end of the semester in May, I got a job tutoring English to Mexican students in the local elementary school. I would work in the mornings and hang out at home in the afternoons. I'd tried to do my best with the green-track program and had been involved in several assembly performances. I did dramatic presentations of Langston Hughes's "Mother to Son" and a monologue from Lorraine Hansberry's *Raisin in the Sun.* Graduation was in June and I had been selected as one of the graduation speakers even though I was a new girl. I was to read an inspirational poem entitled "Don't Quit."

I had been accepted to the accelerated program at Fairfax High School, a special program where I could complete high school in three years instead of four. With California residency, I was sure that I could get into one of the University of California schools. I had my eye on Berkeley.

One day when I got home from work my mother called me from her office and began speaking in Spanish.

"Do you want to go home?" my mother asked.

"I am home," I said. "Where do you think you're calling?"

"No, to where we moved from." She was at work and was being cryptic.

"New York?" I almost screamed with happiness.

"Yes," she said in a secret voice she hadn't used since we'd moved in with my stepfather. "Okay, we'll talk about it when I get home."

It turned out that my mother disliked L.A. as much as I did. She loved the warm weather, but as a Spanish-speaking black person she was an anomaly. She never found a posse of girlfriends to replace the one she had left in New York. In New York, there was a whole Caribbean community for her to be a part of; Los Angeles was strictly divided between Mexicans and American-born blacks, and my mother was neither. She and my stepfather both hated the gangs and the gunshots. My stepfather loved California, but he was willing to give New York a try.

All summer we made arrangements, but by fall we ended up moving to northern New Jersey and not to the city because my stepfather got a job doing electrical work. My mother got her secretarial job at the Wall Street firm back. All summer, I had been looking forward to being back in New York and hooking up with all my friends. Now I was in Rahway, New Jersey, and I was starting all over again.

Things between my stepfather and me were only
getting worse. I'd begun talking back to him, something
I'd always been taught not to do. Sometimes after our
arguments, my mother would go to her room and cry.
"Why are you making me choose sides?" she would say.
To me, there was no choice. I was her child. I had always
been by her side. My brother had left, but I had always
stayed. Now all I could think about was getting to college
and getting away.

Sometimes, my mother and stepfather would go to
the city to go dancing. One night my mother's favorite
salsa band was playing at a big hall. I had stayed home.
The next morning when I walked into the kitchen, I saw
that my mother's head was bandaged the same way as
when my father hit her with the hammer. In the seconds
it took for her to notice I was awake, before she could
explain, I felt my joints lock and my heart begin to flail
with fear and rage. What happened? Why hadn't I heard
anything? Could I do to my stepfather what I'd been unable to do to my father? I was older now and stronger,
but I didn't know if I was braver.

"Last night on the train, there were some kids drink-
ing," she said, motioning me over, trying to get me to
calm down. "One of them threw a bottle and it cut my
head. I'm fine." I was so relieved and yet I felt no less distant from my stepfather.

He and I argued over everything. It would start in the

morning. If I passed him by without a "Good morning" before I brushed my teeth, it was a sign of disrespect. Same if I said "Hi" instead of "Good morning." I hated the way my mother served my stepfather dinner as if he were king. He would ask me to get up and get the salt or the salad dressing from the refrigerator—even if he was sitting within arm's reach. I would refuse and it never failed to start a fight.

One night after dinner, I began helping my mother to clear the table.

"I'm going to wash the dishes in an hour, Mom," I said as I scraped the plates. "I want to watch *The Cosby Show* and *A Different World*."

"Okay," she said, wrapping the leftovers in foil.

"Cecilia," my stepfather called from the living room. "May I speak to you for a second?"

My mother and I looked at each other. I knew that it was the beginning of a fight. My stepfather still rarely spoke to me directly.

"The dishes can't sit while she watches t.v.," he said. "She can't do whatever she wants. Look at how she talks to you! 'I'll wash the dishes later.' She doesn't ask. She just tells you what she wants to do."

I stood in the kitchen, leaning up against the refrigerator as I listened to their conversation. I felt so weak. I hated living in this house. There was no way I could do right. He always managed to see disrespect in everything I said.

My mother came into the kitchen. "Wash the dishes," she said, her voice flat.

"Come on, Mom! You just said it was okay!"

My stepfather came into the kitchen and continued to address my mother. "Look at how she disrespects you! Look at how she talks to you! She's no good. She has no manners. She needs to be broken like a horse."

"Like a horse?" I almost laughed. "You've got to be kidding." I went into my bedroom and slammed the door.

Later that night, my mother called me into the bathroom. "For ten years, I stayed in a marriage that was miserable because of you kids," she said, staring at her own image in the bathroom mirror. "Now I have a chance at happiness and you want to ruin it by being rude. Tono has been talking about leaving, and let me tell you something, if he leaves, then pack your bags and go to your father's. Because I've had it."

I went to my room and cried all night. I was stunned. I knew then that as good as my Spanish was, there were things I'd been missing. For the first time, I felt as separate from my mother as I once had from my father. I hated my father for hitting my mother, my brother, and me. But now my mother had beat the shit out of me with just a few words. In a way, it hurt more than any beating before because I'd trusted her. I'd always believed that no matter what, the two of us would make it. She was the one who talked about not choosing sides, but now it was clear she had chosen.

How could they do this to me? In two years, I would be done with high school and gone. But two years was a long time and I guess he couldn't wait. I knew my stepmother had been rough with my brother. I knew how violent my father could become, but I couldn't see that I had any other choice but to go to my father's house. All I needed was a roof over my head, someplace where I could finish high school. I called my father later that night and asked him if I could live with him. He was ecstatic.

"You don't have to throw me out," I told my mother. "I'm going to Daddy's."

She didn't say a word. And over the next couple of weeks as I prepared to move out, she and my stepfather left me alone. Nobody asked me to do chores. Nobody criticized anything I did. My brother warned me that living with my stepmother was hell, but I didn't entirely believe him. My brother always behaved badly. By the age of twelve, he was a hard-core truant. I figured I could handle my stepmother.

My father was to come for me on a freezing February night. I stood at the window looking at the snow and hoping that maybe, as with his Saturday visits, he wouldn't show up. *Do you really want me to go?* I wanted to ask my mother, but she had become positively glacial, and I was scared to say anything. Earlier in the day, I had packed my one suitcase. My mother hadn't helped me, hadn't said a word as I'd dragged an empty box from the corner store and began to load it with my books.

As angry as I was with her, I could still feel a wave of gratitude when I looked at her face. For fifteen years, my mother had been there for me. More than my father had ever done, she had provided for me. Until my stepfather arrived, I was sure each day and every night that the food I ate, the clothes I wore, the love I received was the best my mother had to offer. If I needed to move out for two years so she could build a relationship, then that's what I would do. I began to tell myself that my moving was a sacrifice I made for her. No one had loved me like my mother. If she wanted me to go, if she needed me to go, then I would leave.

I saw my father's brown Lincoln Continental pull up in front of the building. He began to bang on the horn. I knew he wouldn't get out of the car because my mother refused to let him into the apartment. My stepfather and mother sat side by side on the couch, holding hands tightly. I looked at them and then looked away. It hurt me too much to see how together they were. I looked at her again and silently asked, *What did I do that was this bad?* but her eyes were blank and she didn't speak.

"Good-bye," I said in a fake bright tone.

"Good-bye, Veronica," my stepfather said, gruffly.

"Good-bye, Veronica," my mother repeated like a parrot.

I struggled at the door for a minute trying to carry both the box and the suitcase. Finally, I decided that I needed to make two trips. I took the box down first, then the suitcase. Neither of them moved from the couch to help me. When I came up the second time, I said good-bye again. I wanted to give my mother a hug, but I couldn't move toward her. The space between the door and the sofa seemed so wide then, the carpet was like an ocean. If I waded in too far, I might drown.

"I'll lock the door behind me," I said.

"Leave your keys," my mother said. "I'll lock the door."

I made my way down the stairs carefully with the big and unwieldy suitcase. When I got to the bottom, I heard the lock click into place. From where I stood, I couldn't see whether my mother had been watching me through the peephole. The light in the hallway was dim, I couldn't see very much at all. I stood there for a second and called out "Mom?," but she didn't answer. I opened the door and saw my father in the car. He looked at me and beeped the horn again, for emphasis. He was in a hurry. But I couldn't move fast. I slowly dragged my suitcase across the snow until my father got out of the car and helped me put it into the trunk. Before I could change my mind, we drove away.

six

My father had left Brooklyn and was now living in a town just outside Philadelphia. He'd added banquet manager to his credit as ventriloquist, and was doing a lot of business with the big hotels. He'd been able to move his family—my stepmother, my ten-year-old stepsister, and my four-year-old half brother—to the suburbs. To my surprise, the suburbs of Philadelphia were nothing like the suburbs of New York. It's a largely rural area with lots of farmland. Many of the towns closer to Atlantic City were made up of clusters of townhouse complexes that housed people who worked in the casinos or local businesses, set amidst barren stretches of land.

When we pulled into the circular driveway that led

to my father's townhouse, I felt a rush of excitement at the idea of living in a house again. My father was in good spirits, my stepmother was friendlier than usual. I knew that my father felt triumphant, as if he'd won me away from my mother. I missed her but I had convinced myself on the drive down that this new living arrangement would be the best thing for all of us.

The townhouse had four floors. On the first floor there was a kitchen, dining room, and living room. The master bedroom and bathroom were on the second floor. The third floor had two more bedrooms—a guest room and my little brother's room. The attic, one flight up, had been finished into a bedroom that I was to share with my stepsister.

I enrolled at the local high school just at the other end of the development, my fifth school in as many years. Though I disliked being the new kid again, I didn't have any problem getting into the accelerated program. Once I fed my father the cue about the level of classes I should be in, he made a big production about how his daughter needed to be in the most advanced classes.

My father wasn't around much. He was usually in his office or traveling, doing shows. And I could see that, like the situation with my mother, my stepmother, who worked as a nurse's aide, was responsible for paying the bills on time. By the second month, my stepmother began to grumble about the extra mouth to feed and how I ought to be pulling my weight. I did my chores and kept to my room. By the third month she began to yell at my father about how my mother was "free as a bird" while she was stuck "with that bitch's kids." I started to get nervous.

My mother gave me a toll-free number for her office, because my stepmother said I could no longer make long-distance calls. I called my mother from the pay phones near the principal's office and told her some of the things my stepmother had said and how she would snap at me for no reason. Do your chores and try to stay out of her way, my mother advised me. She promised to send a calling card so I could call her whenever and wherever I wanted. She didn't say I should come back, so I didn't ask, but keeping the talk lines open made me hopeful that things with my mom might eventually work out. Still, I understood now how my brother must have felt when we moved to California without him. Without my mother's invitation, both of us were too hurt and too proud and too scared to ask to come back. I wondered if, on the other end of the line, she felt the same as we did, and if it was holding her back, too.

❧

I started hanging out with the kids in the drama club and got a small part in the spring musical even though I couldn't sing. The high school, although integrated, was sharply divided socially. I had fewer black friends than ever before, since the theater group was mostly white. I knew that some of the black kids thought I was a sellout and sometimes I would hear a couple of the black girls talk about me in the locker room or on line in the cafeteria. "Listen to how she talk," a girl behind me would say and my sentence would hang in the air, unfinished. "She talk like she white. All she hang out with is those white girls."

I knew how my voice sounded by high school. I don't know about elementary or junior high, but by tenth grade, I'd heard enough comments about my way of speaking to know it baffled some, irritated others. "You're from New York?" teachers had said when I moved to Los Angeles. "Funny, you don't have an accent." All the moving, all the different schools had left me without a distinct accent of my own. In L.A., I picked up little California-isms; in New York and New Jersey, too, I absorbed local vernacular. But I didn't think that made me sound white. The proper grammar came from my mother, who spoke English with the precision that only immigrants can. As a child, when I would come home saying "ain't" and peppering my sentences with "I be," "she be," or "we be," my mother would sternly correct me. Plus I read a lot. But I didn't think that it was fair to accuse me of deliberately talking white. I knew that's what some of the black kids thought, but still, I never tried to change the way I spoke to make myself sound more "black." At this point, black slang would have come off sounding even more fake and out of place in my mouth. I didn't let it bother me; I had a group of friends who'd accepted me without questions and I was beginning to feel a part of things at school.

At home, though, things just got worse. My stepmother grew more belligerent, accusing me of absurd things—such as spilling sugar in the kitchen and not cleaning it up—that she knew I would never do. My father was rarely home, but when he was, he never said anything to contradict her. But I'd been down this road before. I wasn't going to ask him to choose. I knew better than to ask him to stand up for me. I'd just stay out of her way.

Play rehearsals kept me busy. I began to write for the school paper and entered any kind of contest there was, as a warm-up for my college scholarship applications— essay contests sponsored by the Rotary Club or the Daughters of the American Revolution, forensic and drama competitions. I was on the debating team, performed monologues, worked on sets, and volunteered for any task that would keep me out of the house.

My stepmother started to accuse me of "running the

streets" and neglecting my chores. A light-skinned woman from Guyana, proud of her fair skin and straight hair, she berated me for being ugly. Day after day, she came down on me about how I looked. It didn't take long for me to believe that it must be true; why else would she be making such a big deal of it? I had always had lots of friends and guys who liked me, but for the first time, I started to feel unattractive. Some of my cousins and kids at school had been into the whole light-skin-and-good-hair routine, but my mother had refused to acknowledge such a pecking order. Black is beautiful, she'd always said, and if I was a good person, there was no way I could be anything but beautiful. At my stepmother's, I found it harder and harder to get out of bed, and I started to suspect that everyone at school thought I was ugly, too.

My stepmother refused to take me to get my hair done, though she took my stepsister regularly. Anyone who knows anything about black hair knows that the straighteners and curly perms require maintenance; if they're not "touched up," the straight hair starts to fall out and the kinky hair starts to grow in. My hair was coming out in clumps. My father promised to take me to the hairdresser, not to worry, but he never did.

I was calling my mother every day from the school pay phone. She listened to the stories about my stepmother and I could tell they were breaking her heart.

Hearing my mother's voice every day became something to look forward to. Away from her daily presence, my mother and I had no reason to fight. "If she's not going to take you to the beauty parlor, try to get your hair cut in a short Afro. That way you can take care of it." At the end of the conversation she would say, "I love you." It was such a simple thing, but I never heard it in my father's house. And when she said it, I knew she meant it.

One Saturday afternoon, I heard my stepmother and her kids getting ready downstairs. I usually stayed in my room until they'd left the house, but I heard my father's voice and hoped that I'd get a chance to ask him for some money after they'd gone. I heard the front door slam and I went to the attic window to watch them drive away. But instead of getting into my stepmother's car, they had gotten into my father's Mercedes and my father drove the whole family away. I saw them that day as I'd never seen them before: They were the perfect little family and nobody would ever know that there was someone missing.

That night when they came home, I called my father upstairs. He made it up two flights—that was as close as he'd come to my room.

"Where did you go today?" I asked him.

"There was a family event at the hotel, so I brought the kids." My father fidgeted in the stairwell, refusing to come upstairs, refusing to meet my eye.

"What about me, Daddy?" I asked him. "I'm your kid. I'm your family."

"This was a business event," he said. "Look at you. Your hair. Your clothes. I can't take you out like that."

I stood at the top of the stairs, staring down at him, wondering if he wanted to hurt me so bad why he didn't just go ahead and knock me down.

"I look this way because of you! You said you'd take me to get my hair done. You said you'd buy me clothes."

"I know," he said, sitting down on the top step. "Next week, I promise."

Next week came and went. The spring play also came and my father did not come to see me. After the play, when all the kids went out with their families, I walked home through the woods. By summer, my step-mother had decided that I was "too ugly and disgusting" to eat at *her* kitchen table, to eat off *her* dishes, or to eat *her* groceries. My father was put in charge of feeding me, which was the same as putting me on a starvation diet because he was never home.

I called my mother. I told her what was going on. She said that I should get my father to take me grocery shopping and to keep some things in my room. I cornered my father one night and got him to buy me some groceries. But in a few days, they ran out and he was nowhere to be found. I waited that night until he came home. It was after twelve and I told him I hadn't eaten

since lunch in school. He drove me to an all-night con-
venience store and we bought a few things. It became a
pattern. I'd load up on food and then I'd have to stake
him out until I could get him to buy me more.

That summer I got a job at a discount clothing store.
The first week I got my paycheck, I was so grateful because I could finally buy myself some food. The next
week, I bought myself some clothes with my employee
discount. I began to think that I could make it, living
with my stepmother.

❦

Before school let out, I developed a crush on a white boy
for the first time. In Brooklyn, in junior high school, I
went steady with a couple of boys: Chuck, who was a
football player, and Trevor, who watched Kara beat me
up and with whom I promptly broke up afterward. In
L.A., I was too scared to go out with any of the guys,
though I did have a crush on a tall, beautiful Wesley
Snipes lookalike named Eric. But I'd never had a crush
on a white boy before, never even thought about it.
Mostly because there weren't any around.

In my predominantly white suburban school, the
theater group was even whiter. The guy I liked was
named Jim. Jim was smart and funny and I thought he
might like me, too. I was excited about going back to

school in the fall, seeing if something might come of it, though I hadn't told any of the white girls because I didn't want them to laugh at me. I didn't want them to tell Jim either. I didn't talk about boys with my mom, because all our conversations were about my father and my stepmother. Besides, we'd never talked about boys before and I wasn't about to introduce the topic now.

Working at the discount store, I met a girl I thought I could confide in. Her name was Joey and she was a black punk-rock girl. She dyed her hair all different colors and wore her sweatshirts ripped and hanging off one shoulder like Jennifer Beals in *Flashdance*. Both of us worked the floor, which meant we walked around, straightening racks and keeping an eye out for shoplifters. I told Joey about Jim and she warned me that I ought to think this crush over very carefully before acting on it.

"Why do you like this guy?" Joey picked up a bunch of T-shirts that someone had thrown on the floor instead of hanging them back up.

"I don't know," I said, pretending to straighten the rack next to her. Our supervisor, Vera, was pretty cool, but you had to at least pretend to be working.

Joey rolled her eyes. "Have you ever kissed a white boy?" she asked me, moving on to another rack.

"No," I said, following her, not even bothering to straighten the clothing. "What's it like?"

Joey made a face like she was about to throw up, fake puking onto the floor. I burst out laughing. "No!" I cackled. "For real?" Joey just kept making sicker and sicker faces with loud barf noises. I didn't stop laughing until we were both lying horizontally under the sales rack, clutching our sides in pain.

"Seriously, is it really different?" I asked as we hung up all the clothes we'd knocked over.

"It's *way* different," she said, sounding very disappointed. Then she put on her woman-of-the-world voice and told me: "Black men are the best lovers in the world."

"Oh yeah?" I asked her, skeptical. "Then why is *your* boyfriend white?"

"Look at my hair!" Joey said, pulling on a bright blue braid. "What black guy would go out with a girl who has hair like this?"

It was true. Black guys did not go for that punk stuff at all. I'd seen the way black guys looked at Joey when we ate lunch together at the McDonald's across the street from the mini-mall. They didn't pay much attention to me, but Joey's colored hair and strange clothes always provoked the most vicious kind of teasing. Still, I wondered why she bothered with her punk get-up if white boys were so heinous.

That fall, I picked up with Jim and the other theater kids again. One day a bunch of us were driving in Jim's truck when he said he needed to pick up something from his house. Construction workers were building another housing complex in Jim's neighborhood and he drove us by the site. He pointed out an area on his left. "They're putting a nigger-ball court up over there," Jim said. The whole car was silent. I was sitting in the back seat with my friend Karen, and I tried to keep my eyes trained out the window. Karen leaned forward and punched Jim in the shoulder. "Jim!" she screeched.

"What?" he said, as if nothing had happened.

"Jim, apologize!" she said again, this time pointing to me.

"For what?" he said, pissed off now. "Veronica's not a nigger."

I didn't hear the rest of the conversation, I don't think there was much of one anyway. But I knew this: my crush was over the minute the word slipped from his lips. I didn't give a fuck how he kissed. I felt stupid for ever liking him in the first place. I was just glad I hadn't told anyone and thank God, the girl I did tell didn't go to my school.

∽

A new girl moved onto our block. Her name was Stacey and she saved my life junior year. We were nothing alike. She was model-beautiful, tall, and athletic. She played basketball and ran track and ran with a totally different crowd. But she had come from a messed-up family situation and when she saw what the deal was with my stepmother, she completely understood what I was going through. I never felt comfortable telling the kids at school everything that was going on, but I didn't have to tell Stacey. She practically lived next door, she could see it.

Stacey, her mother, and her aunt practically adopted me. Stacey tried to teach me all the beauty tricks I'd never learned. "Come over in the morning before school and I'll knock some curls in your head," she would say. She was a wizard with a curling iron. In the evening, if my father wasn't home, I would eat at her house. My father learned to look for me over there, and even though she was only seventeen, just a year older than me, Stacey had no qualms about telling my father he needed to give me money for food or for my hair. And most of the time, he would do it. I was amazed at the way he just forked it over when Stacey was around. Stacey had that effect on people. Especially men.

When things got really bad at home, I'd sleep over at Stacey's. If, for some reason, I couldn't stay there, I would go to my theater teacher Miss Blake's house. One night after rehearsal, when everyone had gone home and we were cleaning up, I'd told Miss Blake what was going on at home. She was young, twenty-seven, so we all felt comfortable hanging out with her. At the same time, I started to feel like I had to talk about what was going on with a grown-up. It was getting harder and harder to live at home, and I was growing afraid to go back there every night.

"I would hate to see you leave this school," Miss Blake said. "But isn't there someplace else you could go?"

"No," I said, dragging the folded chairs to the backstage storage room. It made me nervous to open up to a teacher, especially a white teacher. I didn't want her to start feeling sorry for me.

"Well, if you need a place to stay any night, give me a call and I'll come pick you up."

"Thanks," I said, turning around quickly.

Miss Blake never mentioned my problems at home in front of other students. And even when she would invite me to see a play or go out to dinner, it was never a pityfest. I soon trusted her enough to call her when I needed a place to stay. But on the nights when I felt ashamed of spending too much time over there, I would just walk down the highway until I thought my stepmother might be asleep. Then I would turn around and go home.

Those nights spent on the highway I learned to walk close to the brush and would will myself into invisibility. I thought about my mother and knew that she was at home, sleeping. Although I always told my mother about the things my father and stepmother did, I never told her about the nights like these. I didn't want her to be afraid for me, even though I was afraid for myself. A few times truckers would offer me rides and I knew it was only God's good graces that made them move on when I said no, I didn't need a ride. I remembered the prayer that my mother had taught me and my brother, the Twenty-third Psalm. I would say it over and over again. It was the only psalm that I'd ever learned by heart. It made me feel close to her, though I couldn't ask to come home, couldn't summon the words, couldn't make my mouth say them. But on the highway, walking in the darkness, I curled into the space my mother had carved in my heart.

❧

My stepmother's best friend was a woman named Janey. Every couple of weeks, Janey would come to visit, always loaded with presents for my stepsister and half brother. I would stand by, trying to concentrate on some chore. After passing out the presents, this woman would turn to me and smile. "And how are you, dear?" she would say in a thick West Indian accent that sung to me of islands I'd never visited and my mother's circle of friends in Brooklyn. Janey's voice made me nostalgic for the bossy but loving Esmerelda. Janey's smile, the singsong of her voice, took me back to my mother's house, to the women laughing around the kitchen table.

Secretly, I believed this woman was my silent ally (she called me *dear*, didn't she?), that in private she would admonish my stepmother to stop her abuse. "Take it easy on the girl," I could almost hear her saying as I sat in the attic room, straining to hear the conversation downstairs. I imagined that this woman was my advocate, if not my savior. At the very least, I thought she would bear witness to the screaming and deprivation that my father allowed.

I needed a witness because we had few guests and I was losing my grip on reality. If things got worse this woman would say something. She would step in. She would call somebody. But she never did.

Talking to my mother always made me feel better, but it was the things she didn't say—"Come home, I'm coming to get you right now"—that made me realize I was on my own. My mother was not going to rescue me. She never visited me at my father's house, and never asked me to visit her. When I told her about the violence in the house, she would tell me, "You'll make it. Everything will be okay," or, more often than not, she would just listen in silence. I thought of the time when I was little when my mother walked me all the way to my father's apartment in Brooklyn. "Don't you threaten my daughter!" she had said. Why now did she not say a word? Why didn't she ever call my father on any of the things he did? "I can't tell someone else how to run their house," she said. She made it clear: when I left her house, I lost the right to her protection.

That year, I turned sixteen. My birthday, as expected, was a nonevent in the house. My stepmother did not acknowledge it. My half brother was only five and didn't know it was my birthday. My stepsister whispered "Happy birthday," out of her mother's earshot. My father said nothing. My mother sent me a card with a spiritual message about strength and growth. I propped the card up on my dresser and read it before I went to school every day.

The morning of my birthday, I walked over to Stacey's house so that she could "knock a few curls" into my head before we left for school. As I passed the house next door to Stacey's, the guy who lived there opened his door. Don was nineteen and Sri Lankan. He lived with several of his cousins, all male, in a townhouse on our block. He was tall and athletic, a tennis player. He attended the local state college. I'd gotten to know Don a little bit just from talking in front of our houses. He never asked me on a date, though I sensed that he had a crush on me.

"Vicki," he said, calling me by the name my family used. He had heard my stepsister refer to me as Vicki and had used it ever since.

I walked up to his door. "Happy birthday!" he said in his sweet British accent.

"Thank you." I smiled.

"Stacey told me it was your birthday," he said. "But I didn't know what to get you because I didn't know what a girl would like. I was thinking maybe after school, you'd come with me to the mall and pick something out."

I didn't know what to say. He remembered my birthday *and* he wanted to buy me something. Amazing. I considered the fact that Don might expect me to put out in exchange for the present, then dismissed the idea. He was even more shy than I was.

"Okay," I said. "I get out of school at two-thirty." We agreed to meet in front of his house at three.

I went to Stacey's house and she gave me a beautiful pair of silver earrings. I told her about Don and she told me about how she'd coached him through the whole thing. By the time I got to school, I'd begun to feel really good about sixteen.

I met Don in front of his house, as planned. We got into his car, a little orange MG, and drove to the mall. "I just got a credit card," he said. "So you'll help me break it in." We headed straight for the clothing stores and after half an hour, I picked out a sweater.

"Is this too expensive?" He looked at the price tag and shook his head no.

"Why don't you pick out a skirt, too?" he said. So I did. Then we went to the food court and got something to eat. Don told me about going to school in London and how prejudiced he felt the city was. Putting his arm next to mine, he said, "I'm black like you are, you know. Sri Lanka or Africa, it makes no difference." I asked him to tell me about his college and I told him about my plans to go away to a big school. "You're smart," he said. "You'll do just fine."

When I got home, my stepmother was in the kitchen cooking dinner. She said nothing to me as I walked past her up to my attic room in silence. A few minutes later, my stepsister came upstairs and said, "Did you get out of Don's car?" I told her yes. "Did he buy you that stuff?" I told her yes. She said I was lucky that a guy that cool liked me. "I know," I told her. She went downstairs to have dinner with her mother and I started working on my homework. I was taking honors biology and it was kicking my ass.

Around eight o'clock my father came home. "Vicki!" I heard him scream from the bottom of the stairs. I pretended that I didn't hear him. "Vicki!" he called again. Then it occurred to me that it was my birthday and maybe he had a present waiting for me downstairs after all. I walked down to the kitchen, nervous and excited. But when I saw the look on my father's face, I knew there would be no cake. He was eating the dinner that my stepmother had reheated for him. I wondered how he could eat so heartily. He knew my stepmother refused to feed me, refused to have me keep my groceries in her refrigerator, refused to let me eat off her plates.

"Sit down," he said. My stepmother sat silently next to him with a smirk on her face.

"What is this I hear about some man buying you clothes and driving you around in his car?" he said.

"What are you talking about?" I said, sitting at the kitchen table, my heart beating volubly.

"I know that some man bought you clothes today and dropped you off in his car." He stabbed a piece of lasagna and put it in his mouth.

"You mean Don? Don who lives right down the block? He's a college student and it's my birthday." Where was this going?

My father stood up and took off his belt. I felt real fear then. What I felt before was pre-fear, an appetizer to the hearty serving of terror that now pulsed through me. My father hadn't hit me for years. For *years*. Now he stood above me, with a belt in his hand and a wild look in his eyes.

"What are you doing to this man for him to be buying you things?" he hissed accusingly.

"Nothing, Daddy," I whispered.

Then he hit me across the head with the belt and started screaming, "Don't lie to me! Don't lie to me!" My stepmother sat at the table as if she were in the stands at a polo match. With her back straight and her hands crossed in front of her, she seemed that serene, that elegant. My father, in comparison, began to beat me in a crazy haphazard fashion.

"Don't lie to me!" he said. "Don't lie to me! You filthy, fucking whore!"

He knocked me off the chair and I huddled on the ground, trying to protect my head with my hands. But when he said *whore* I'd turned toward him and the belt came down again, right across my face. *Whore?* I was a virgin. It had been a good two years since I'd made out with a boy. When Don dropped me off, I'd kissed him on the cheek. I was a whore?

I tried to run for the stairs, but he pulled me back. As the blows came down in a regular rhythm, I began to feel tired, like I would pass out and he would just keep on beating me. I decided I had to make a run for the door. Surely he wouldn't follow me outside and beat me in front of the neighbors. I took a deep breath, stood up, and ran for the door, which was luckily unlocked. But I was wrong, my father felt no shame in following me outside.

The townhouses on our street were situated around a cul de sac. I made it as far as the circular driveway before my father knocked me down again. "Whore! You filthy fucking whore! This isn't what I raised you to be! How dare you disrespect me in my house!" I thought that maybe one of the neighbors would see and call the police, but if anyone was watching, they were silent. I looked over to Don's house and saw his car was gone. He was at work. He worked nights at a gas station in town. I had to make it to Stacey's.

I ran for her door and pounded on it. Her aunt opened it immediately and I fell inside. She looked out and saw my father standing in the street with the belt in his hand, his shirt and tie disheveled. She closed the door and I spent the night there.

I went home that morning to shower and change for school. No one said anything to me and I didn't feel afraid. I knew the worst was over. I tried to cover the bruise on my face with foundation, my jeans covered the bruises on my legs, which were far worse. I wore the sweater Don had bought me and I was grateful that nobody—not my father nor my stepmother—said a word to me.

I called my mom at lunchtime and told her everything. She cursed at my father. She asked me if I could make it one more year.

A year? Was she serious? What if I said no? Would she come for me then, would she take me back to her house? I never found out because I told her yes, I could make it another year, it would be all right. I began to suspect that on some level my mother saw all this as my punishment for leaving her house. If I wanted to act like a grown woman, I had to learn how to take grown-woman blows. I said yes, I could make it, because I felt like that was the only grown-up answer I could give. I'd been wrong to leave my mother's house. My mouth had written a check that my behind had to cash.

That afternoon at school a message came over the PA system telling me to report to the principal's office. There, waiting for me, was a messenger with a bouquet of helium balloons, all saying *Happy Birthday* and tied with pink string. The note read, "Happy Birthday, Daddy." I trembled with rage as I threw the note away. Walking back into the classroom with the balloons, I felt humiliated, ridiculous. My classmates ooh-ed and aah-ed. "Is it your birthday?" they asked.

"Yesterday," I told them.

"Well, whoever sent these really wanted to make up for forgetting your birthday, I guess," the girl next to me said.

"Something like that," I said. Did he think these balloons would make up for yesterday's beating? He was crazy. But this was just like all the times he didn't give me lunch money, only to personally deliver a pizza to school. My father did the most evil things behind closed doors, but when he was trying to be nice, he wanted as many people as possible to know about it.

~

My stepmother became harder and harder to ignore. What had been a weekly harangue was now a daily routine of screaming and accusations. By May, I became afraid that I wouldn't make it through the next year. A girl named Sarah, who lived in a trailer park, had heard about my situation and asked me if I wanted to get an apartment with her and her boyfriend. Sarah spent all her time at her boyfriend's and the two of them drank pretty heavily. Sarah was no scholar, she was a party girl, and I was afraid that if I moved in with her, I'd lose sight of school. I thanked her, but declined.

I had fallen into a routine that was difficult, but manageable. I was making honor roll every semester, performing in plays, and working at a restaurant. I was never hungry anymore because I ate at the restaurant and took leftovers home. I loved the restaurant work—arriving at four and setting up tables silently with the other waitresses, being so busy at six that before you knew it, it was twelve and the manager was dividing up tips. I would walk out the door at midnight with a pocketful of cash and a doggie bag. I'd learned how to ignore my stepmother and though she screamed every day, it didn't get to me the way it used to.

But all these sad scraps that made up my life were getting to me in a different way. I kept wanting to give in, to cry in somebody's arms, but I couldn't. In school, we'd learned about Georges Seurat and our art teacher had gone on and on about pointillism. But the paintings overwhelmed me in a way that had nothing to do with art appreciation. I felt like inside I was just so many dots. From a distance they blended together to make a picture—complete and whole. But up close, the dots were all disconnected, and I felt that at any moment, I would lose my composition. I would explode all over the place, like a handful of confetti thrown in the air. From the abuse I took to the way I was shutting down every emotion just to survive, I was becoming just like my mother. I thought school would save me, make things different, but somehow I was in the same place she was.

I had all these rules I'd made to ensure that I would make it to college and not get sidetracked. I wouldn't drink, not even a taste. I wouldn't smoke a joint or do any harder drugs. I would not sleep with boys. But I knew that I was getting to the place where I couldn't keep up this schedule much longer and obey all these rules. I was getting to the point where I didn't give a fuck.

I made an appointment to see Ms. Chatmon, my counselor. We sat down and considered my options. She told me about a program called A Better Chance that enabled minority students to attend private boarding schools or live in a house with other students while attending a good public school. She said she would help me fill out the application and send it in. She suggested I try to get into one of the historically black colleges under an early admissions program and offered to call Howard and Spelman. The University of Chicago, she mentioned, also had a history of accepting early college students.

After the PSATs, I had received daily bundles of mail from colleges. Most of them I threw away, but there was one brochure for a school called Simon's Rock College that I'd kept in the pile underneath my bed. *Why Wait to Go to College?* it asked me. Simon's Rock was an early college that accepted students after the tenth or eleventh grade. I showed the brochure to Ms. Chatmon and she thought it sounded like a good idea. She allowed me to use her office phone to make the long-distance call to Massachusetts to request an application.

I told my mother about my conversations with Ms. Chatmon and, as usual, she offered no opinion. She didn't say she was against it, but she didn't say she was for it. It made me so mad. I was trying to save myself. Why was she acting like she couldn't care less?

"What do you think I ought to do?" I asked.

"I don't know," she said. "It's your life. I can't live it for you."

I already knew that was her position, she'd made that clear in every conversation we'd had over the past year and a half, whether she'd said it or not. She also knew that I was independent enough that, whatever she said, I was going to do what I thought was right anyway. Still, what I wanted to hear was that she cared enough about

me to offer up her two cents. But she wasn't about to. I
was on my own, there was no going back, that was the
message all along.

❧

The junior and senior prom was fast approaching. Don
was my date. We still hadn't done more than kiss lightly
on the lips, but I liked it that way. If he'd pushed for
more, I would have had to dump him. I couldn't deal
with more, there was too much going on. Although I
was working at the restaurant, I didn't have much money
saved. Not enough for a prom dress. As always in matters
of fashion, I turned to Stacey. "I've got the perfect dress
for you to wear," she said. "Come to my house after
school."

When she took the dress out of the closet, I felt like
Cinderella meeting her fairy godmother for the first time.
It was white satin, with a mermaid shape that accentu-
ated the hips I did not yet have. It was a one-shoulder-
style dress that I'd seen in fashion magazines. With the
money I had saved, I bought a pair of white shoes and
white stockings. I was going to be fine for the prom, I
wasn't going to look like anybody's stepchild.

I told my mother about the prom, Don, Stacey's
dress. "I wish you could see it," I said.

"Me, too," she said, and I could hear the distance in

her voice. There was so much we would never share. Talking on the phone every day had made us something like loyal pen pals, but we were never going to have those touchy-feely mother-daughter Hallmark moments. I thought about how my mother never knew her mother. Together, we had a chance to make up for everything that death had stolen from her when she was so young— how could she not want to seize it? How could she screw this up?

The evening of the prom, I went to Stacey's house to get ready. Stacey, her mother, and her aunt began to fuss over me. They did my hair, my makeup, my nails. It was so exciting, but I wished my mother was there helping me get ready. As much as I loved Stacey's family, I felt so alone. But soon our dates arrived and I told myself, Just for tonight, forget everything, have a good time. And I did. Don took out the beautiful corsage he had bought for me and Stacey's aunt began taking pictures. He fumbled to pin the corsage to my dress, so nervous that his hand was in proximity to my breast. I just laughed. I laughed the whole night.

A few weeks later, I received a letter from Simon's Rock requesting an in-person interview with me and my parents. I was completely bummed. I took the letter to school and kept folding and unfolding it. I would have to tell my father. I called him at work so we could talk privately, away from my stepmother. To my surprise, he was thrilled with the idea. He said he would call the school and make an appointment for the next week. I realized then two things: One, that my father was thrilled because if I went to college early, my stepmother would be off his back, and two, if I waited for him to call the school, I could be waiting for months. "No," I said. "*I'll* call the school and make the appointment."

The following Monday, my father and I set out for Simon's Rock. In the car, my father gave me a tired song and dance about how glad he was we were able to spend time together, how my stepmother was a bitch, and how he was going to "put her in check." The five-hour drive was excruciatingly slow. But when we arrived at Simon's Rock, I came to life. Our student guide was an African girl named Valerie. She was beautiful, smart, and funny and made me feel welcome. She told me that the freshman dorms got loud and that if I decided to come to Simon's Rock, I should feel free to visit her and her friends in the upper-class dorms.

At the interview, the college admissions director asked me a bunch of questions, all of which my father tried to answer for me. "She's always been bright," my father boasted. "She reads two or three books a week." I looked at him and felt nothing but bitterness.

The admissions director finally said, "Mr. Chambers, perhaps you should let your daughter talk." He looked at me and asked me why I wanted to leave high school, why I wanted to come to college early. He told me that it wouldn't work if I was trying to run away from problems at home. Of course, that was exactly what I was doing. I wanted out so badly, I'd read the college catalogue hundreds of times; I could recite whole passages in my sleep. Instead I told him, "I've always been in accelerated classes and I really like school. I hadn't planned on coming to college early, but when I received the brochure, the slogan 'Why wait to go to college?' caught my eye. I've got so many credits in high school that all I'll need to take senior year is gym and English."

"That's a common occurrence," he said, smiling approvingly. "But of course, there's the prom. Won't you miss going to the prom?"

"I went to the prom this year." It was so close now, I knew . . . "I don't need to go again."

He talked to us about scholarships and financial aid and then we headed back home. A week later, I received an acceptance letter in the mail. The first week of June, there was another package waiting for me when I came home from school. It was from Choate Rosemary Hall. My application to A Better Chance had not asked me to indicate which boarding school I would like to attend, but here in my hand was an acceptance letter from Choate along with an application for financial aid. Three years before in L.A., I'd spent weeks dreaming about going to Choate, but now it was too late. I was going to college.

Stacey was going to Rutgers University in the fall. "You little nerd," she said. "I can't believe you're not going to have to suffer through senior year like I did." I was going to miss her and I hoped we would keep in touch. I planned to start working full-time at the restaurant in a few weeks when classes ended. I could save a lot of money and buy some really fly back-to-school clothes.

A few days after the school year ended, I was sitting in my room, reading. It was a Saturday afternoon and I didn't have to be at work until four P.M. My stepmother came stomping up the stairs. My heart jumped; I knew what that stomp meant. She was in a mood and she was looking for me.

"Did you take my Sunday paper, Vicki?" she asked, her hand on the banister. Her face was contorted in anger.

"No," I said, sitting up in the bed. Thank God, I thought, I don't have to take your shit for much longer.

"What's this?" she said, taking the paper out of the garbage can in the room.

"I didn't bring it up here," I told her, and she knew it. I was so afraid of her that I would not touch anything that belonged to her. I knew that's what made her so mad. I was always so obedient, it was hard for her to come up with reasons to yell at me.

"Liar!" she screamed, charging toward me.

"Don't scream at me," I said evenly. The acceptance letter from Simon's Rock sat in my dresser drawer. I tried to imagine it now, the exact words they used that told me I was going to make it.

She was two inches away from me now. "Liar! Thief!" she screamed. Then she slapped me. I tried to move out of her way, but she pulled me down the stairs. I screamed for my father, who for once was home. She came after me, grabbing at my shoulders, my face, my neck, and I began to choke. Her eyes were cold, distant, and I knew in this wild gesture, she was trying to hurt my mother, too. She'd spent her whole marriage denigrating my mother, as if the prize of her husband, my father, was not enough.

She began punching me and I thought of an old schoolyard threat, *I'll hit you so hard your mama will feel it.* When I had the fight with Kara, my mother had told me, "Nobody can fight for you, but you." But I'd become used to just taking the blows and I never learned how to fight back. She was pummeling me for last Sunday's paper on Saturday with a new paper on the way. For all I knew, she could have put the paper in my room. How were you supposed to defend yourself against that?

We tumbled down another flight of stairs and I heard my father's thick footsteps. *This won't last,* I whispered to myself. *He's here.* But the steady stream of blows was so confident, I feared she had no intention of stopping. I glimpsed my father's face and I knew he had already chosen a side. Not mine.

"I refuse to get into this," he said. Moving aside, he stood at the top of the stairwell watching us.

"Daddy," I cried. "Daddy, *help me!*"

"I refuse to get into this," he repeated, as if this were an even match or a barroom brawl, out of control.

And it seemed like my stepmother laughed then. I can't imagine that she would have, but it is how I remember it. What I do remember is the glint of her teeth before a sharp pain unlike any other exploded in my arm. All my life, like my mother, I had been afraid of dogs. I was always afraid that some big, barking dog would attack me. Now I was being attacked by a woman and it was too surreal. I became convinced that I was sleeping, that I was dreaming my worst nightmare. I had dreamed of her before, my stepmother had long before replaced the bogey man as the monster of my nights. But when I looked at my father, I knew it wasn't a nightmare. It was worse because it was real and I was screaming "Daddy, help me, Daddy, help me," and he would not. I kept calling for him and he just stood there watching. And the pain of that was worse than the pain of being beaten. For all his shortcomings, I had never imagined my father to be this cruel.

My stepmother kept her grip on my arm for what seemed like forever. Like a tongue searching for a wobbly tooth, all the nerve endings in my body were alive and on fire. It was as if my whole body could be swallowed by this one bleeding space—it hurt that badly. I became convinced that if not attended to, I would bleed to death. My stepmother's punches became relegated to the distant borders of my skin, while inside, I tried to figure out what to do about the wound on my arm and the blood that was gushing through it. Had she ruptured an artery? I'd gotten a B+ in honors biology, why couldn't I figure it out?

I felt tired and let my body be hit, lifeless. Only my voice would not quit, I kept calling for my father to save me. But then eerily it all added up: I had thought so often of running away, but I never really knew what it promised until this moment that told me it was so bad that anywhere beyond the front door was better than here and now.

I broke free and ran toward the door. I stopped screaming for my father and started screaming for the police. My father suddenly flew into action. "Sssshhh, sssssh," he half spoke and half spat, reaching to put his arm around me as I bounded toward the door. Then he began yelling when on the doorstep I would not stay in his embrace.

"Don't you dare call the police. I will *never ever* speak to you again," he bellowed as I ran to Stacey's.

I didn't care. I turned around and screamed at him, "I'm pressing charges. I'm going to the police."

"Don't tell!" he said, as if the scene we were creating in the middle of the street could somehow be contained. "Don't you dare!"

I held my arm trying to stop the blood. I ran to Stacey's. My father faded in and out, soft then loud, over the ringing in my head.

"*Please* don't call the police," he said softly.

I didn't answer him.

"Don't you *dare* call the fucking police!" he yelled.

That's the way it was, all the way to Stacey's house. Please and fuck and please and fuck and please and fuck. Stacey and her aunt bandaged my arm, my father returned to his house. A short while later, he came back to Stacey's with a bag of my things, pounded on the door, and announced that he was driving me to the bus terminal. I was to spend the rest of the summer at my aunt Diana's, until I started Simon's Rock.

"I'll work this out," he said on the way. "I'm going to go home and deal with that crazy bitch." I stared out the window. I'd heard so many lies. "Don't tell," he whispered. "Don't worry. Don't tell." His words circled around my head like annoying flies. Now he wanted me to start telling lies, too.

I got on the bus with one small bag. My father

promised to bring me the rest of my things in a few days. Another lie. My stepmother threw away everything I owned. All my photos, all my clothes, all my books, books I'd been collecting since the first grade! My stuffed animals, my honor roll certificates, gone. When my father showed up at my aunt's house two weeks later, I rushed to the car and because the back seat was empty, I told him to pop the trunk. The trunk was empty, too. I would start college in two months. I had nothing.

I say nothing. I don't tell. I don't dare tell. Nobody helped me before, I told myself, nobody needs to hear my sob story now. I was free of it. I convinced myself that's all that mattered. So I kept secrets for people whom I owed no favors. I let the words commit suicide, before they were given breath. My words are meaningless. My father watched as I begged for help. My words are powerless. The little I had is gone. What I have left are new words, so I will try again to write a new story.

seven

The first thing I did when I arrived at my aunt's house was call my mother. She seemed shocked by the story I told her, but she didn't rush over to see me. "I'll come soon," she said. "The important thing is that you're out of there." On the phone, I made agreeing noises, but inside I wanted so badly for her to come hold me, to take care of me. Throughout the summer, I would see my mom on the occasional weekend, but mostly I met her during the week at her office and she'd take me to lunch. I spent most of my days with my cousin Guille, who'd just had a baby and had moved into the basement apartment with her boyfriend. I tried to look for restaurant work, but a lot of places turned me down, saying I didn't have enough experience. Finally, in August, I got a job working the 5:30 A.M. shift as a busgirl at a coffee shop in Rockefeller Center.

I asked my family for little. I knew that things were tight with my mother. My stepfather had been laid off from his electrician's job and my mom was handling most of the bills. Still, she tried to help me the best she could. Along with my aunt Diana and my aunt Veronica, she made a list of the absolute essentials I might need at school. They all chipped in and bought me sweaters and flannel nightgowns, snow boots, sheets, a blanket, a hotpot, an iron, and a clock radio to ensure that I made it to class on time. "Plus," my aunt Diana reasoned, "you'll have something to listen to."

Yet when it came time to see me off, my mother pulled away. Over the phone, I asked her to come see me the night before I left for school, but she refused. "You don't need me to supervise your packing," she said. "Just make sure everything is clean and don't forget to roll. You'll fit more in that way." I was so hurt, I begged her to come see me off, but she wouldn't. I used to wonder what I had said or done to anger her, but now, when I realized she wasn't going to cave in to my pleas, I said good-bye and hung up the phone. Now that my dream was coming true—I was going to college—it felt like she was still trying to hold me back, that she still thought I was wrong to "push myself ahead."

My father had agreed to drive me to school. He had also agreed to pay the remaining tuition that my scholarship did not cover. It was blood money, I knew, in exchange for not pressing charges against my stepmother. I didn't care. My mother had no money at all; if I had to ask her for it, I wasn't going to college.

The day of our departure, my father called and said he had car trouble and wouldn't be able to drive me to school. "Rent a car!" I told him. "I need to get to school today."

"I've got to stay down here and get the car fixed," he said. "I'll wire you the money to take the bus."

"But how am I going to get to Port Authority with all my stuff?" I asked, trying not to cry, feeling so stupid that I'd entrusted the most important day of my life to someone as irresponsible as my father. "I've got a suitcase, but there are all these bags with my blanket, my hotpot, my school supplies. I can't take the subway with all this junk."

"I'll arrange for a ride," he said. "I'll call you right back."

I didn't know if he'd ever call back, so I called my mother at work. She said to give him an hour, then I should get my cousin Guille and her boyfriend to call me a cab. Exactly an hour later, my father called.

"A friend of mine who owns a limo service is going to give you a ride to the bus station," my father said, an excited tone in his voice.

"What time will he be here?" I asked. A limo sounded cool, but if my father's friend was as unreliable as he was, I might miss my bus.

"Didn't you hear what I said?" my father asked, upset now. "I'm sending a limo to take my baby girl up to college. You're traveling in style."

I didn't care about traveling in style. I just wanted to get on the road, away from all the bullshit both my parents were visiting on me.

The limo arrived right on time. My cousin and her boyfriend were totally excited about it and deep down inside, I had to admit that its slick black elegance gave me a rush, too. But when my father's friend got out of the car, he sneered at my shopping bags. He was an older West Indian man and I could tell he did not approve of me or my packing abilities. I had one suitcase, but whatever didn't fit, I had put into doubled shopping bags.

"Gee-yall you nah have no shame?" he asked. "Going up to di white man's school with all your tings in plastic bags like a street rat." I couldn't answer him. I was trying so hard not to cry.

In the car, he made it clear that we were not to make ourselves at home. "Don't touch a damn ting!" he said, glaring into the rearview mirror. When he dropped us off at Port Authority, he didn't say good-bye or good luck. He just turned around, got back into his limo, and drove away. My cousin and her boyfriend walked me to the

gate and helped me load my things in the hatch underneath the bus. I took a book and my knapsack and settled
in for the ride to Massachusetts.

The bus took Route 7 through Connecticut. It was
a slow, beautiful drive. When my father and I had driven
to Simon's Rock, we took the Taconic Parkway—pure
highway all the way. Looking out the window, I was
amazed at the beauty of the late summer. Driving into
the Berkshires, I began to realize all that lay ahead of me
and what I was leaving behind. I wasn't happy with the
way things were with my mother or my father. I knew
my mother had done more for me than my father, but
when she hurt me, it was worse. My mother was a mys-
tery. She was at once responsible and caring but she so
easily left me out in the cold. Which is, I thought to myself, why you are on this bus alone. At least I was going to
make it to college.

Once I settled into school, I was deliriously happy. I
picked my courses, I got a job in the kitchen, I was in a
dorm. I resumed the habit of calling my mother every
day. She sounded relieved that I was finally content and in
a place that was safe, if unfamiliar, though she never artic-
ulated this. I was called by more than one upper-class student "that overly friendly freshman." It was true, I smiled
all the time. I felt like I had a lot to be happy about.

Walking into the Simon's Rock dining room, I
couldn't help but think how different it was than the high

schools I'd attended where fights broke out all the time. In this little educational oasis, I knew that fistfights probably never happened. I could tell that these were girls who never had to fight. I could count the black girls on my two hands and the white girls, for all their revolutionary speak, looked decidedly soft to me.

In elementary school, there was a rhyme that all the kids would say when a black kid got into a fight with a white kid:

> *A fight, a fight,*
> *A nigger and a white.*
> *If the black don't win,*
> *THEN WE ALL JUMP IN!*

At the schools I attended, the black kid always won. But I thought of this rhyme, as crude as it was, several times at Simon's Rock. I knew that even in all my wimpiness, I could take on any of these girls and more importantly, the prospect of such fights was negligible. But the second part of the rhyme, the part about "we all jump in," was about more than a simple fistfight. It was about having your "peoples" to look out for you, to "watch your back." And if I ever felt alone at rough, black schools, that feeling was doubled at Simon's Rock.

At the same time, Simon's Rock gave me the space

to claim a blackness that I did not think belonged to me in Brooklyn. In my college classes, as much as I hated being the "black spokesperson," that role made me think every day of the community I had left behind. I began to talk and write about my experiences at home, what I had seen and what it all meant.

Still, throughout my first year, I began to grow frustrated about being the "token minority" on campus. In my childhood, especially during Black History Day and later Black History Month, I had learned about Booker T. Washington, W. E. B. Du Bois, Mary McLeod Bethune—all the great black educators, and how prized the greatly educated were. But at Simon's Rock, there were no black teachers, there was no black staff, and the college was situated in the middle of an overwhelmingly white small town.

"What did you expect?" my mother said. "You went up there and visited. Did you think miraculously they would create a whole black population just for you?"

"I never thought about it," I admitted.

"Ah . . ." my mother would say, in that annoying way she had of letting me know that I'd have to work things out for myself. I'd been so busy thinking about getting into college early, I never even thought about the racial makeup of the school. My tour guide, Valerie, had been black and that's all I noticed. Now that I was actually enrolled, I had a lot more time to think about what being one of twelve black students on a campus of three hundred really meant.

Among the black women posse at school—Angie, Karen, Valerie, and me—there was a strong sisterhood that I hadn't had since my double-dutch days. I started spending time in the "mod" townhouse where these girls lived. They were sophomores and their housing was a step above my freshman dorm. Hanging out with them, I used vocabulary that I had always felt afraid to use at home. Angie, Karen, and Valerie were special because they were each top students but they could also get down. They laughed at me for being stiff, but they also made me feel comfortable.

Back home, I had always felt too shy to dance. Every black party was like a mini-episode of *Soul Train*—boys and girls looking good and shaking their groove thang. The dances that filtered through New York to Atlanta to Chicago to Los Angeles and back around again came and went so quickly. By the time I learned a dance it was on its way out. Every party was cause for scrutiny and even if I attempted a new dance in the corner where nobody was looking, some bigmouth was sure to say, "Ooo girl, check it out. Veronica is getting down with the wop." Then I'd get embarrassed and stop.

Simon's Rock dances were a joke, as I learned during the orientation week "jam." First of all, you spent the better part of the evening convincing the so-called DJ to play some up-to-date rap music, not just the Run-DMC cover of Aerosmith's "Walk This Way." Then, once the tunes started bumping, there was no way any dance you did could be wrong. It seemed like the white students were dancing to completely different music. The long-haired, hippie-girl "modern" dancers actually twirled their skirts and made shapes during Hammer's "Can't Touch This." Other kids slam-danced to everything from Madonna to Young MC.

I would call my mother and describe this scene to her. I made the stories elaborate and colorful and I loved to hear her voice laughing on the phone. When I told her about how the white kids were slam-dancing to Bob Marley's "No Woman, No Cry," we both laughed so hard I thought we'd never stop.

When I hung out with Angie, Karen, and Valerie, I loved the way we addressed each other: it was always "girlfriend," "sis," "flygirl." We punctuated our stories with "Chile, please" and "Honey, let me tell you." It made me remember that I was the girl who had stomped around Beverly Road answering the call of "Oooh, she thinks she's fine" with a resounding "Baby, I *know* I'm fine." When girls like the ones in L.A. and Brooklyn stepped to me and wanted to fight, I never felt the need to speak their language. I never saw myself in them. But I saw myself in Angie, Karen, and Valerie. As isolated as we were at Simon's Rock, the language became a way of plugging us back into our hometowns. The words were warm and comfortable, like connectors to the darkest and most beautiful parts of myself, and when I reached out to them, I felt electric and alive.

It felt good to be able to call my mother and share with her all my new experiences. I tried to keep in touch with my father, but if I called his house, my stepmother would hang up the phone. If I called him at the office, he would sometimes not return my call for weeks. My mother might get on my nerves sometimes, but that first semester at college, I began to realize that she was all I really had.

After the second month at school, my father stopped sending my tuition checks. I was called to the financial aid office and told I wouldn't be able to attend classes until I straightened it out. I told them that my mother had no money and I didn't know what to do. Thankfully, it was a small school and even though I was a freshman, I'd already gotten a good reputation. I was freshman class representative to the Community Council and I was doing well in my classes. I had been named a W. E. B. Du Bois Scholar. After a few days, the financial aid officer told me that I was eligible to apply for another loan, but I would have to work to make up the rest I owed. I was already working in the kitchen, but I signed up for tutoring and a job at the library, too. Between classes, Community Council, the People of Color Coalition, and working, I was exhausted.

I would call my mother every day before my first class. Sometimes she was sympathetic, other times she would get a major attitude. "I never sent you to that school," she would say. "You sent yourself because you thought you were a grown woman. If you lived with me, you would have gone where I could afford. You would be at Brooklyn College and you wouldn't be killing yourself." I knew that was my mother's way of saying that she hated feeling so helpless. All my life I'd wanted more and she'd always told me to be careful, not to aim so high. I guess one of the reasons was because she didn't want to be in the position of seeing me reach for the stars and being unable to lift me up.

My mother did what she could. The first few weeks, I saw other students getting care packages from their parents. "Mom, do you know what a care package is?" I asked her. She didn't. "It's a box that parents send to kids with food and clothes and candy and stuff."

She said, "I'll see what I can do."

Two weeks later, I'd forgotten all about our conversation when I was told there was a package for me at the switchboard. I ran down the hill to the college center, wondering what it could be. The box was huge and I almost cried when I saw the address in my mother's handwriting. Diane, the switchboard operator, gave me a pair of scissors and I ripped the box open right there. There was a new set of sheets, a box of hot chocolate, several different kinds of tea, caramel popcorn, and a letter with a ten-dollar bill inside. "I'll try and send you what I can every payday so you don't have to ask for it," my mother wrote. I clutched the note tightly in my hand and closed my eyes. I missed her.

eight

I am ten and my brother is seven. Our mother works. From three P.M. to five P.M. we go to the after-school center in the basement of P.S. 152. There we paint and make things. Then at five we walk home together. Our mother will be home soon and she'll make us dinner and we'll tell her about our day. In East Flatbush where we live, the neighborhood changes at six P.M. It takes our nine-to-five parents exactly an hour to get home. Between five and six, we run around each other's houses though we're forbidden to have company, we go outside when we're supposed to stay in as punishment, we plug in the t.v. though our parents have unplugged it. At six, order is restored.

It is fall and it gets dark earlier. I am afraid of the dark, of the possibilities that lurk on the seven blocks between school and our house. But my brother is younger and it's important that he doesn't know that I am scared. My brother and I walk together, talking about our favorite t.v. shows, *The Facts of Life* and *Diff'rent Strokes.* He doesn't let me hold his hand. At seven, he says he's too old. But I pull his shoulder when we get to the corner. I look both ways before I nudge him across the street.

On the third block, walking toward us, an Asian girl is holding hands with a white boy. I imagine they are heading to Midwood High School, which is just a few blocks away from our elementary school, or to Brooklyn College, which is also close. They are teenagers, and I am impressed with their age and their romance. But then I hear cursing behind me. From behind us, four white guys push their way toward the couple. They push the girl onto the sidewalk and then begin to pummel the boy against a tree. One of the guys has a knife and he cuts the boyfriend across the nose. As the silver blade meets the boy's white skin, opening it like a change purse, pools of blood spilling like coins onto the sidewalk, he says, "Why can't you stick to your own kind? Why can't you stick to your own kind?"

∽

I knew of only one interracial couple growing up. My friend Maxine's mother dated a white guy by the name of Rocky. Rocky was the only white man who lived on our block. We hardly ever saw him, he came in late at night and left early in the morning. He was never around on Saturdays, but was sometimes there on Sunday afternoons. My mother never said anything about Rocky, but I noticed that she wasn't particularly chummy with Maxine's mother, Clarice. I got the feeling that she thought Clarice was social-climbing with Rocky, that maybe for Clarice, black men weren't good enough. My mother and all her friends dated only black men.

When Maxine and her brother Ian had money, we knew Rocky had been around. Rocky never left their house without leaving some money on the kitchen table. Sometimes Ian would wake up earlier than his mother and steal a few singles off the wad. Clarice was a beautiful West Indian woman in her late thirties when I knew her. Rocky was older, in his fifties, with salt and pepper hair, tall and thin. I did not know how they met or how they ended up together. It never crossed my mind for a single second that they were in love.

∾

When I was a kid, there was a black Barbie, but not yet a black Ken. It was not something that I questioned; it was in a way a mirror of our homes. Black mommies, but so few black daddies. Now that I am older, I wonder what was going on in the corporate boardrooms at Mattel. Why was there a black Barbie and no black Ken? Was black Barbie a test of doll integration, a girl alone like Linda Brown in 1954 wading into a white classroom? Was the idea of a black Ken too menacing? Was there a prototype, and did it look like Richard Roundtree in *Shaft?* Or was it much more genteel, a "Look who's coming to dinner, Barbie" Sidney Poitier–type in brown plastic? Did the creative execs grimace at the thought of how to make a black Ken anatomically correct?

I wonder now if black Barbie, like the glamour figures of our day—Diahann Carroll, Diana Ross, Lena Horne—was expected to transcend race and become betrothed to white Ken. I never thought about white boys before high school and my nigger-ball experience. In elementary school, white girls were always a fascination because of their straight hair and because it was white girls who were featured in all the advertisements we saw for clothes and toys. White boys were a nonentity; no girl on my block ever, ever owned a white Ken. Without black boyfriends, the black Barbies made do with each other.

❧

I always imagined that in college, I would meet the *Ebony* man of my dreams. At Simon's Rock, there were five black men and seven black women and I figured out pretty quickly that as long as I stayed at this school, it just wasn't happening. Still, I spent my Saturday afternoons cutting pictures out of magazines to decorate my dorm room—Vernon Reid of Living Colour, Terence Trent D'Arby, Michael Jordan. I knew that eventually I'd meet a guy who was as beautiful and talented as these guys, and if I had to wait a while, so be it. I spent so many Friday nights hanging out at the mods with Valerie, Karen, and Angie. We would cook pasta while listening to Sade. We would croon "Sweetest Taboo" to each other, pretending to be sexy, tortured torch singers. We would get all dressed up and talk about the pitiful selection of black guys on campus and all the fine black men we'd known at home. We talked about whether or not we would date white guys. We weighed the pros and cons and talked about which white guys we thought were cute. We had so much fun those nights. And although Simon's Rock didn't offer much in the way of social life, none of us transferred after sophomore year like some of the other black students did. We all stayed there for four years because we had each other and because the school, with its corny dances and negligible black population, had grown on us and become our home.

I went to work that first summer at Goldman, Sachs,

the brokerage firm where my mother had worked for many years. She had arranged for me to get a summer job through their college student program. Although she and I had grown closer over the year and I could be civil with my stepfather, I decided not to stay with them in New Jersey during the summer. I was more comfortable living with my aunt Diana in Brooklyn. She had been like a second mother to me, and living in Brooklyn, as opposed to Jersey, meant my friends and I could hit the clubs at night without worrying about missing the last bus home.

The job at Goldman, Sachs was a boon. I made more money that summer than I had ever made. I was bored stiff, working as a receptionist and forbidden to crack a magazine, much less a book. But I was a full-time paid employee and that made me very happy. I loved being able to see my mother every day and have lunch together. We would talk about the people in the office and I understood so much more about why, when I was little, my mother seemed tired all the time. These people would work her to the bone. It was different for me, I was one of a few college interns and nobody expected much of us. They knew we were in college and that one day, if we came back, it would be as colleagues. We wouldn't be answering their phones or making their photocopies. Over lunch, my mother would laugh at the way I made fun of the company.

"Be glad you don't have to spend the rest of your life

here," she joked with a tinge of resignation. What we both knew but left unsaid was that just one year at college promised me a life beyond the secretarial pool that engulfed her every day.

My best friend that summer was Brian, a Simon's Rock classmate. My mother, my aunt, and my cousin Guille referred to him as "Brian, the white boy," but still my mother really liked him; I don't know why, but that surprised me. The same qualities I appreciated in him— his friendliness, his adventurousness, his sick sense of humor—my mother liked, too. I wondered sometimes if it was the novelty of his whiteness that she liked. My mother had grown up during the civil rights era, but still she had no white friends. The only white people I ever heard her mention were the people she worked for. Brian was different. He wasn't my boss, he was my friend, an intimate. I called him names, caught an attitude with him when I was ready, and I felt no fear. I think in a way it was fascinating for my mother to be able to see me as an equal to a white man.

My brother was still living with my aunt and cousins though they had moved from Brooklyn to Long Island. He was fourteen that summer and we didn't talk much. It had been so long since we lived together, so long since we'd been within visiting distance, that we had very little to say to each other. I knew from my mother that he was still flunking out of school. When I talked to him, he only wanted to talk about being a rapper. I knew my mother was worried about him, but I was tired of worrying about my brother when he didn't seem to give a damn about himself. I was seventeen and I had my own life to think about.

Toward the end of the summer one of the guys from the mailroom asked me out. Ray and I went to the movies and afterward, he walked me home to my aunt's house. We sat on the porch and talked. I told him about school and he told me about his dream of one day returning to Goldman as a stockbroker. We dated for the rest of the summer. I introduced him to my mom and he was polite and charming. As they say in Brooklyn, he had good home training. When I was getting ready to go back to school, I tried to get Ray to promise to come visit me.

"You wouldn't want me up at your school," he said one day when we were having lunch near the office.

"Why?" I refused to believe that this relationship would end by Labor Day and I'd go back to being a black spinster up at school. "It's so dead up there. I'd *love* for you to visit me."

But Ray went on and on about how I wouldn't want to be with a mailroom guy in front of my college friends. I had tried to convince myself that because he talked about going back to school and getting a degree, we were alike. But what I didn't understand was that the fact that I was in college, that I never had to drop out of school to work, put me in a far different place than Ray. If I hadn't gone away to school, if I had stayed in Brooklyn and was working as a secretary like my mom, then our dreaming together of a better life would have been less artificial. But sitting across from him in a diner, I somehow couldn't see how different we already were. I had spent years dreaming about going away to college, but before my freshman year, I'd never spent a moment thinking that college might change me and, in the changing, I might grow apart from my mom, my brother, and guys like Ray.

~

The first semester of my sophomore year went quickly. I was taking twenty credits and working as many work-study jobs as I could squeeze in. I began to think of becoming a political science major and fulfilling my mother's dream of becoming a lawyer. That semester, I tutored a girl named Samantha in Spanish. I knew Samantha because she used to hang out with "Brian, the white boy." Samanatha was a writer and had won several poetry contests in teen magazines like *YM* and *Seventeen*.

Samantha had spent the summer working at *YM* and from the sound of it, she'd had a lot more fun than I did at Goldman, Sachs. In the safety of Simon's Rock, I was able to dream about more than just surviving. Sam suggested I try to get an internship at a magazine. I spoke to my advisor and he said it was worth a try since I probably wouldn't be able to get a meaningful legal internship until law school.

In Brooklyn, over October break, I sat with a copy of the New York telephone book and called every magazine I had ever heard of. Every one of them blew me off. But when I got to S, I decided to call *Sassy*, a new teen magazine. I was connected to a helpful woman who told me to send her my résumé. Back at school, I went into action. I put together a résumé, following instructions from a book in the library. I wrote a cover letter asking if the magazine would consider me for an internship during my four-week January break. A few weeks later, I called the woman and we scheduled an interview around Thanksgiving when I would be back in New York.

I called my mom to tell her about it and although she didn't seem particularly excited by the idea of working for a magazine, she gave me advice about how to handle the interview.

"Wear a skirt," my mother said with authority in her voice. Twenty years as a secretary on Wall Street made protocol one of my mother's specialties.

"Yes, ma'am," I said, laughing. "What kind of questions do you think they're going to ask me?"

"You're a student. They'll ask you about what you're studying and what you want to do with your life."

"Doesn't sound too bad."

"Don't slouch!" she said. "And don't say 'huh?' every five seconds. You do that all the time."

"Huh?" I said. We both laughed at my stupid joke.

A few days after the interview, I was offered the internship. I was so excited. I hadn't met much of the staff during the interview, but I loved the hustle and pace of the office. I didn't know what went on every day at Goldman, Sachs, but I could see what they were doing at *Sassy* whenever I picked up the magazine on the newsstand.

I called my mom to tell her the good news and when she asked me how much the internship paid, I remembered the bad news. The internship didn't pay. I would get four credits.

"How are you going to eat?" my mother asked. "How are you going to buy tokens?"

I asked my mother if she would give me lunch money and train fare as a Christmas present and she agreed. It would be my first Christmas present in four years.

I had a blast working at *Sassy*. Being a teenager at a teen magazine gave me an authority I'd never known before. And even though I did drudgery, like transcribing tapes of interviews with Keanu Reeves, it was glamorous drudgery.

I applied for and was offered an internship at *Seventeen* for the spring. I spent the entire semester in New

York. That summer, I got an internship at *Essence* and I was starting to get the idea that what I wanted to do was work at a magazine, not go to law school. I was still staying at my aunt Diana's and talked to my mother every day, meeting her for lunch or dinner when I could.

One evening, I called my mother and my stepfather told me she wasn't home. I left a message, but she didn't call me back. The next evening, I called back again and then again, only to have my stepfather tell me repeatedly she wasn't there.

"Well, where is she?" I was worried; my mother had never not returned my call.

"She's out," he said, evasively.

"Well, tell her to call me when she gets home," I said. "It doesn't matter how late."

When she still hadn't called me, I went into a panic and told my aunt that I hadn't heard from my mother in three days and I was really worried. My aunt told me that my mother was in the hospital having surgery and didn't want me to know. My aunt and I made up to meet after work and go to the hospital together.

As we walked to the hospital, my aunt told me that my mother had fibroids. One of them was as big as a four-month fetus. My aunt tried to explain that my mother didn't tell me because she didn't want me to worry. It was driving me crazy the way my mother would swing back and forth—first telling me that I had to look out for myself and be a grown woman and then, when she's so sick that she's in the hospital, keeping it a big secret, as if I couldn't handle it. I planned on telling my mother off, telling her that she couldn't treat me like a child anymore, but when I saw her I forgot everything I wanted to say.

My mother, who was thirty-eight, suddenly looked fifty-eight, and worse than any time that my father beat her up. She was weak and thin. Her warm chocolate skin was ashen and chalky-looking, though her voice was the same.

"Hi, Poops," she said when she saw me, using her favorite good-mood greeting.

"Hi," I said, but I hung back, unable to make myself go to her. She looked so very different.

My aunt suggested that we take my mother for a walk down the corridor. Walking was supposed to be good for her, but my mother was in too much pain to get out of bed. Her face contorted when we tried to move her. I thought then of all that she had kept hidden from me and how at this moment her face betrayed her and she couldn't hide anymore.

"Why didn't you tell me?" I blurted out through fresh tears. I didn't want to cry, didn't want her to have to comfort me when she was in so much pain.

"I didn't want you to worry. You're always so worried," she said. I watched my stepfather enter the room and take the seat across from my mother's bed. He was so clearly terrified, and for the first time, I saw how much he loved her. My aunt was like my mother; efficient and responsible, she never fell apart unnecessarily. I realized this is the way most everyone in my family is—nobody has the time, money, energy, or space to fall apart. I was the only person in the room who couldn't stop crying and I knew that this was considered a weakness and that's why they hadn't told me. My tears, like my college education, made me different.

My mother left the hospital a week later. By the end of the summer, she was back to herself. But inside, both of us had changed. I knew that she was saddened by the fact that she wouldn't be able to have children with my stepfather. And when I kissed her good-bye before I left for school in the fall, I was reminded of her mortality and how much I loved her.

❧

The next summer, I got a job at *Life* magazine. I had started taking photography classes and was excited about working at *Life* because of their amazing history of photographers. I had completed my junior year at Simon's Rock and I could hardly believe that I had only one year left. When I got to my aunt's, there was a phone message from *Glamour* magazine saying I had been chosen as one

of their Top Ten College Women of 1990. I'd forgotten
that I'd entered the contest—I entered and applied for
everything—but I was so thrilled to have actually won
this particular one.

Glamour sent a photographer to take a picture of me
at Life and with all of the lights and activity, I attracted a
little more attention than an intern on her first week of
the job should. There was a weekend of events in August
and my mother took me shopping in anticipation of it.
Even though I was earning decent money at my internship, my mother insisted on buying me clothes—an
Armani-style blazer and skirts and blouses to "mix and
match." For the awards ceremony, she bought me a beautiful gold silk dress. At the register, my mouth fell to the
floor when the cashier presented my mother with the
total. I tried to offer her money, but she declined and just
smiled at me. I knew she was proud of me. After years of
me shoving my straight A's in her face, of trying to show
off my double-dutch moves, after her being too tired,
too busy, too wrapped up with my brother, she had finally focused on me and I made her proud. Maybe it was
the feeling of relief that moved her, relief that accompa-
nied the realization that there would be no more teary
phone calls about my father and stepmother, that I was
safe at school and that in this strange world of magazines,
a world she didn't know and couldn't understand, I
might have a chance at success.

Still, for all the good things that were happening in my life, I felt weighted down by a heavy sadness. I lost my appetite. I found it impossible to sleep. I stayed up at night reading. I watched reruns of *The Odd Couple* and *The Honeymooners*. I ironed my clothes at two in the morning. I walked in circles around my little room in my aunt's house.

I was afraid to sleep, afraid of the darkness and the quiet and all the emotions that for the last three years of college, I'd tried to keep in check. I felt like I couldn't complain about feeling tired, about feeling like I was always on my own without a safety net because *look how far I'd gotten!* But I wasn't happy. I lay in the bed with the light on, my Walkman on, and headphones over my ears. I listened to sad-voiced women singing sad songs—Sade, Anita Baker, Billie Holiday.

"Vicki?" my aunt said, and the sound of her voice made me jump. "Why are the lights on? It's four o'clock in the morning."

"I'm sorry," I said, getting up to turn them off. "I can't sleep."

I got used to the dark circles under my eyes, circles darker even than my mahogany skin. *You ain't nothing but a hound dog,* I mumbled under my breath as I got dressed for work, covering my eyes with dark sunglasses.

I went to work and came home again and headed straight for the kitchen to get the dog's leash. Walking my aunt's dog was one of my chores. I didn't mind, I didn't even mind having to clean up after the dog. Walking, and sometimes running, with the dog was the only exercise I got.

As I approached the kitchen, I was shocked to hear my mother's voice. It was mid-week, so she must have come to my aunt's house straight from work. It was strange—my aunt didn't mention that my mother was coming over. Although my mother and my aunt were sisters, neither operated an open house. We always called before visiting, that's just the way it was done. Something must be wrong, I realized. I took a deep breath and gave my mother a kiss. What is it now? I wondered.

"Can I talk to you upstairs?" she said, and I was sure it must be about my brother. My brother had dropped out of high school earlier that year. He said he was going to pursue a career as a rapper, but none of us knew what he intended to do until his big break. He refused to go back to school and after so many years of his flunking and being a perpetual truant, my parents had just given up.

It was odd to see my mother in my room. It had been five years since I lived in her house. She had never visited me at my father's. She had never visited me at college. When she came to my aunt's house, she usually stayed downstairs. Her being in my room felt ultra-personal. Impulsively, I started to make up the bed.

"Sit down," she said. I took a seat on the floor beside

her. I didn't know why we were on the floor. We had both come from work, we were both wearing dresses, stockings, and heels. I looked at my mother's legs and wondered if she was wearing the same shade of coffee Hanes as mine.

"What's going on?" I asked.

"D says you're not sleeping?" she asked. I was the reason she had come. I couldn't believe it.

"Insomnia," I said, looking away.

"She also says you're not eating." She looked at me, worried.

"Anorexia," I joked. She didn't laugh. In fact, she looked horrified.

"What?" she said sternly.

"I'm just kidding," I said. "I only said anorexia because it rhymes with insomnia. I was being flip, I'm sorry." I didn't know how to deal with all her attention. The pow-wows in our family were never about me. I'd always wanted to be at the center of the family drama and now I had a major case of stage fright.

"What's wrong?" she asked again. She said it patiently and kindly, not in the hurried, harangued voice that I grew up with.

"I'm fine," I said. "Just a little down in the dumps. You better go, you've got to catch a bus."

"Don't worry about my bus," she said. Then she

reached over and hugged me. She hugged me and did not let go. This was not how we hugged. Our hugs were quick, an addendum to saying good-bye. This hug was different. It was not a hug about going away. It felt so strange, so strange it didn't really feel good. Why this, why now? Was I dying? Was she dying? Then my mother started to rock me, rock me like I wanted her to when I was seven and terrified of my father, when I was ten and afraid of living in a strange new apartment building, when I was fourteen and walking out of her front door.

I was so afraid that this was not real that I didn't dare hold on to her. My arms fell limply at my sides. If this was just another dream, I didn't want to wake up with my arms wrapped around thin air, rocking myself.

I never thought she'd do it. I never thought she'd see how much I needed it. I started to cry, I figured it was okay to cry now.

"What's going on?" my mother asked.

"I'm not so strong," I said. "You always thought I was so strong. I'm trying to do everything—do internships, go to school, get good grades, pay for school. I can't do it all. I don't know how long I can do it all."

"I hope you're not doing all that to impress me," she said. "Because I always told you and your brother just to get your high school diploma. You can sell flowers on the street for all I care."

"That's the whole problem!" I cried. "You don't care until something goes wrong. The more good I do, the more you ignore me."

"That's not true," she said, looking genuinely shocked. "You know how proud I am of you."

"You signed my report cards without ever looking at them," I told her slowly, dragging out hurts more than ten years old.

"They were always A's," she said. "I didn't have to look to know that. I was always so thankful that you weren't in trouble like your brother. I was so glad I didn't need to worry about you."

"Worry about me, Mom," I said. "Start worrying about me."

We talked like that for hours. All my life, I'd hoped to meet someone upon whom I could unload everything. The best friend who would take my side completely. The boyfriend who would shelter and protect me. It never occurred to me that my mother was the person I wished for. I thought she was lost to me. I thought we were by now too different, that too much time had passed and that it was too late to make those requests, too late to lean on her. I'd assumed she'd known everything I'd felt and just didn't care. But I was wrong and I was thrilled to be wrong.

In my mother's arms that night, I found a safe space. I was a child again and being a child didn't make me feel weak or afraid like it did when I was a girl, helpless to protect my mother or myself. In my mother's arms, I found healing.

That night, I walked my mother to the door and again, she embraced me and again, her tight embrace felt foreign. But I smiled because it was a strange thing I wanted to get used to. As she held me, I thought of the book *Beloved* resting on my dresser upstairs. I thought of how the mother, who was an escaped slave, rather than seeing her daughter returned to slavery, killed her own child. But in the novel, the child returns to her mother from the dead. We must all make our peace, I thought. I felt lucky to have made mine in life and not through the murky swamp that separates life from death. She is my beloved, I thought, watching my mother walk down the street, her form retreating into the coming darkness.

nine

In two weeks, my brother Malcolm will be twenty-one. Right now, he is sitting in jail. I am sitting in my cubicle at *The New York Times* where I am an editor. If there is a worse place to receive this information, I can't think of it. When my twelve-year-old half brother calls me with the news, I must curl over my desk and whisper into the headset. All around me are white faces, no one that I can turn to and say, "You know, my brother's been arrested—I've got to go." Lucky, then, that it is almost five and I can just pack up my stuff and leave.

At home, I call my mother, who calls my father. I stopped speaking to my father three years earlier when I decided I had had enough of all the drama. My father still lives near Philadelphia, where my brother has been arrested. The week that my brother is in jail, we play this weird game of telephone—my brother talks to my father, who talks to my mother, who talks to me. At first my mother and I are extremely calm, we discuss the details with a clinical detachment. This is not the first time my brother has been arrested. It's about the millionth time that we've pow-wowed over Malcolm and wondered, What should we do, what should we do?

But the evening news sets me on edge—I see my brother in every young black man. Just as prejudiced as some white people, I find myself thinking, *They all look alike!* It amazes me that however many hundreds of years after the Diaspora and a splitting apart of a people, the family ties between black men and women are so visually evident. But that's too easy. The deeper issue is that the resemblance between my brother and all these other young black men bothers me because I'm wondering, *How will* they *know this is my brother? How will* they *know not to hurt him?* I think of another black man, Alexandre Dumas, and his tales of the Three Musketeers. Set within the context of the inner city, Dumas's motto, "All for one and one for all," has scary connotations for young black men. You go, I go. And every other street corner has a story about how Peter took the bullet for Paul. I spend the better part of the night crying, as I always do, hot and heavy, angry tears.

Just the week before, I'd spoken to Malcolm. He was

living with his girlfriend, a twenty-year-old woman with two kids, neither of whom were his. "How are you eating?" I asked him. He told me that his girlfriend got food stamps. His answer implied that he wasn't dealing drugs anymore. I didn't like the idea of my brother living on welfare, but since he had a complete aversion to working for minimum wage, I decided not to push it.

Once I'd gotten out of college, I'd joined my mother in the crusade to save my brother. I grew up with the understanding that the world is a harder place for black men than it is for black women. That it is easier for a black woman to get a job than it is for a black man. I knew there was a way that the world made black men angry and that as a black woman, you worked around it, you kept your cool, you kept things together.

After five years of frustration, though, my mother and I had recently made a pact to restrict our efforts to words of support and guidance and not to give my brother any more cash because it never seemed to do any good and it might even have done some harm. If he wanted to live off a girlfriend's welfare, that was his business. But it turned out that was just another lie and now he was in jail. My mother and I guessed it was a drug offense and we were right: possession with intent to distribute. It was a charge that sounded familiar, like something I'd seen on a rerun of *Miami Vice*.

My cousin Guille, streetwise and familiar with the

territory my brother had made his home, warned me to stop worrying about him. "He's out there doing what he wants to do," she said. "Malcolm doesn't care about anyone but himself. He'd take your last dollar, your rent money, your food money, and he wouldn't think twice about it. Look out for yourself."

But the success I had found in journalism made it hard not to wish my brother would find similar satisfaction in his life. Once again I was the super sister, thinking of what I could do to help him, and then I thought of the red winter coat and my heart hardened a little bit.

A year before I joined *The New York Times* I was living and working in Los Angeles. I hadn't heard from my brother for almost six months. He was hard to track down. He shuttled between Atlantic City and New York, living with different friends and different girlfriends. He wasn't good about letting me or my mother know his current phone number and address. The last phone number I had for him was a beeper number that didn't work.

In early December, my brother calls me. He is in Atlantic City again. It's already begun to snow back East. My brother says he does not have a winter coat and is walking around in a denim jacket. He wants to know, could I send him money for a coat? I remember our pact and tell him that I will send him an actual coat instead.

It's odd to go winter-coat shopping in southern California. Not that it doesn't get cold at night, but it's never so cold that you have to bundle up in layers. As I walk through the mall, feeling coats for bulk, checking the labels to see if they are water-resistant, considering colors, I think about winters when I was small. My mother would get up first, shower, and get dressed. She would turn on the oven and leave the door open to warm up the tiny kitchen. Our apartments were always freezing and we couldn't afford space heaters. My mother would wrap my brother and me up in a blanket, walking us through the cold apartment into the bathroom. We'd take quick showers, then my mother would walk us back to the kitchen where she'd have our clothes laid out in front of the oven. I loved how warm the clothes felt against my skin, the turtleneck and jeans toasty from the oven's heat. It wasn't something I thought about, this ritual of warmth. I thought everyone got dressed in front of the oven in the winter and I assumed it was something I would do for the rest of my life.

It wasn't until college, my junior year, when I lived in an on-campus house, that I had the opportunity to adjust the heat in my room for the very first time. I kept the thermostat at 80°. My roommate was a white girl from the Midwest who loved the fresh air so much that she insisted on keeping the windows open, even during the brutal Massachusetts winter.

"You can always put on more clothes," she said, padding around in her Birkenstocks and socks.

"I *can't* get warm enough," I told her. I wanted it so

hot that I was sweating. I wanted it so hot that I could sleep with only a sheet even in the middle of December. I wanted to explain to this girl about the cold apartments I grew up in, to tell her about getting dressed in front of the oven and the way my mother would boil tea for us at night so that we were warm enough to sleep. I wanted to explain what heat meant to me, how I had to have it, how I had to control it, but I never did. I didn't want her pity more than I wanted the heat.

I think of this girl and the oven and my mom when I am shopping for a coat for my brother. I buy him the biggest, most expensive red coat I can find.

I tell my mother about the coat, about the Christmas package I'd put together for Malcolm of CDs, a book, and the coat. My mother has just moved to Miami with my stepfather. She is still looking for a job and doesn't have much money. She asks if she can split the cost of the coat with me and make it a joint Christmas present. I agree and sign a card with both our names, though the truth is, I will never ask for her half of the money.

I leave my office early and take the package to the post office the next afternoon. I circle the block until I find a parking spot close to the front door. I lug the box out of the hatchback. A young guy dressed in a suit and tie holds the door for me. He looks like one of the budding studio execs that work in the mailroom at Columbia Pictures, just across the street. I push the package near the windows, then stand patiently in line. It is two or three weeks before Christmas, but I know that Christmas mail can be slow and I don't want my brother to be presentless on Christmas Day.

I am called to window #1. The thirtyish guy behind the counter is from South Central. He has a Gheri curl and a Snoop Doggy Dogg drawl. I like him because he keeps pictures of his beautiful baby daughters by his window and he calls me ma'am. He laughs when he sees the pitiful job I have done trying to seal the box with masking tape. "What did I tell you about this cheap tape?" he says, taking out the industrial-strength good stuff from beneath his desk. "You're lucky you got me and I'm gonna help you out. But do me a favor. Treat yourself to some good quality tape for Christmas, okay?" I laugh and agree.

"Malcolm X. Chambers," he says, reading the label. "That's a helluva name. Is this a present for a man out East?"

I shake my head. "Nah, it's for my little brother." I smile at him. There is something about this guy that just makes my day.

"Have a good one, ma'am," he says. I wish him the same and speed back to my office.

I remember it all so clearly even though it was just one of many gifts I was able to give that season, one of the many trips I took to the post office, one of a million errands to run before I took off for Christmas. It is so clear in my memory because it was one of those rare days when you just feel infused with love. I still believed that loving my brother would help see him through the mess he'd made of his life.

I spend Christmas in Miami with my mother. Not a word from my brother. Neither my mother nor I know how to get in touch with him. New Year's also goes by without a peep. Then sometime in early January, he calls me. "What's up, V?" he says, in that slow guttural delivery that so many guys like him have—an urban panther's growl.

"Malcolm!!!" I screech in what my brother calls my black Valley Girl speak. "Where have you been? What's going on? Why haven't you called?"

He pauses. "Yo, I've been busy. It's rough out here, V."

I don't want to ask because I don't want him to feel that I'm being obnoxious, but I can't help it. "Did you get the coat?"

He pauses again. "Yeah, the coat. Yeah, it was phat. But yo, it was too small so I gave it to my friend 'cause you know, he's smaller than me."

"You did what?" I hiss, barely audible.

"It was too small so I gave it to my friend." The tone in his voice warns me not to push the point any further.

I'm trying to think how not to turn this into a fight. I'm trying to think how to keep my cool. It's been almost a month since my brother's last call and if I piss him off, it could be months before he calls again. "Malcolm," I say as calmly as I can manage. "Malcolm, that coat was an extra-large. How could it not fit?"

My brother sucks his teeth. He knows this conversation is going to drag on and he's not pleased. "Yo, it fits in the shoulders and stuff, right?" he says, lapsing into a sweeter, more explanatory tone. "But the sleeves were too short. And V, I ain't got no gloves."

Whenever we were kids and we tried to outsmart my mom, she always used to turn to us and say, "I was small, too, you know. I wasn't born big. I was your same size and I had your same sneaky thoughts." Sitting on the phone with my brother, I'm thinking the same thing. He must take me for a real fool. Not only do my mother and I buy him this really nice coat that he says he needs badly, he doesn't call to wish us a Merry Christmas or a Happy New Year, let alone thank us. He gives the coat away. No gloves. Please. He lied. He wanted money and instead he got a coat he didn't need or want.

∾

Now my brother is in jail and I am home in my apartment. I can't sleep. I'm having nightmares. I think about my brother all day, can't shut him off and do my work. I want to ask for a leave of absence at work, but I know that I can't. I am one of only two black editors. There is a constant and incredible pressure for me to succeed. A leave of absence opens the door for talk of incompetence. I can't explain to the people I work with where I've come from, what I'm dealing with. I don't think they would understand. Honestly, I don't think they want to know.

My brother's girlfriend calls to inform me of the prison's visiting hours. I tell her I'll try to make it, but I don't know how. This is one of those times I wish I worked at a factory or that I pushed papers at some nameless, faceless place where nobody cares where you came from or what you're about. But I don't. I have a career. So I am relieved at the end of the week when my brother is released from jail.

A month later, I go to visit my mother for the Fourth of July weekend. We are on the beach and we are wearing matching swimsuits. The day before, we were running around the mall like teenagers, trying to stay one step ahead of my stepfather and my boyfriend. We raced over to the swimsuits on sale. I had taken one over to my mother—cream with mesh netting that I thought would look good against my brown skin. "What do you think of this?" I'd asked her. She turned, laughing. She was holding the same suit. We'd each offered to choose another—dressing alike seems a little too Mommy Dearest—but we loved the design and after my mother pointed out that we live in separate states, we agreed to dress like twins, just for the day.

The waves are crashing hard. It is hurricane season and the ocean is temperamental. My mother still has not learned how to swim. Neither have I. The four of us— two men, two women—stand just a few feet in, jumping the waves when they come, splashing each other in between, until the rain forces us indoors.

In the house, my mother and I sit at the table and talk. The conversation turns inevitably to my brother. Despite all the things we have worked out, how we relate to my brother is the one thing that always makes me feel like I can't stand her. There is a saying that black women mother their sons and raise their daughters; when it comes to my mother, the saying is too true. My mother raised me—there were a lot of hard times, times when we both were hurt and angry, nevertheless I am the woman I am today because of her. But my mother let my brother walk all over her ever since he was a child. Her way of looking after Malcolm was something I'd emulated, not only out of concern for my brother, but to please my mother. Eventually, though, I became so fed up that I got tougher on him. I felt sympathy and wanted to support Malcolm and all the young brothers in his situation. But unlike my mother and the black women of my childhood, I wasn't going to support a black man at the expense of myself. This realization changed everything about how I viewed Malcolm, how I viewed my mother, and how I viewed my father. It was like we were all playing this black woman–black man game and then I moved my piece right off the board.

"If I could do things differently," she says, her voice small and helpless, "I would've been more strict with you children."

I cannot hide my frustration. My fists are clenched, my whole body is stiff. The same rain that we were dashing through a few moments before is giving me a migraine. Although he is twenty-one, she still considers him the measuring stick by which she will be judged as a mother. If he straightens up and does well, she will consider herself a good mother. If he never gets his act together, she will be a failure. So many times I've tried to explain to my mother that there is a difference between circumstance and choice. My brother and I grew up under the same circumstances, but we made a million different choices along the way. The circumstances we could not control, but the choices were ours to make.

"You do your best," my mother is saying. She doesn't listen to what I tell her, and I hate it when she ignores me like this. But the truth is, the same advice I give her, I still find hard to follow. This is one of the things that makes us so much alike. I tell her she's not a failure because of what my brother does or does not do. Yet I feel like I won't ever be able to enjoy my life fully, to enjoy my successes without guilt as long as my brother is out there dealing drugs and getting arrested and beginning to think of jail as a second home.

Once when I was in college, I went swimming alone. It was early spring, March, barely warm enough to go in the water, late in the day, sunset. I went swimming alone though I can barely swim, not knowing even how deep the sublime campus river was. I waded into the cool water, deeper and deeper until I got a cramp in my leg and felt myself being pulled under. I was pulled under a footbridge as the dusk of late afternoon turned into the pitch black of night. I could not stay up. My wet palms slid along the mud wall of the riverbank. I felt myself falling and then resigned myself to falling, tired from the struggle. Then I decided to shout. I felt I had to try and shout. So I pushed up and screamed. I screamed again, though my head was full of water and it sounded like a whisper. I was screaming and whispering at the same time. Then I saw someone, then I couldn't see and only felt someone. Then I was lying on the side of the river. Wet and cold, but alive.

I know my brother is out there swimming. I know that he can barely swim. I know that the day is darkening on him. I know that he is sometimes tugged under because he can disappear for weeks on end. I know that he is resigned to falling in. I know that he thinks he will survive as a ghetto merman but he is falling in. I know that in water oxygen is finite. I know that he may come up this time or next, but there may come a time when he does not come up at all.

I know what it's like to nearly drown. When your arms are tired and your legs are dead weight. When your body betrays you and there is nothing and no one to hang on to. Even now I can still summon the fear. And what I fear more than anything is that if my brother spires to the surface, if in a moment of clarity he shouts and it only comes out as a whisper, will anyone hear him? Will anyone help him? Will I be able to hear or help? Or will he, resigned and tired, sink back to the bottomless bottom?

My brother at three was practically mute; he refused to speak until he was almost four years old. He spoke only through me, some strange gibberish that I cannot now recall. Now that my brother is a big strong black man, with big strapping black man problems, I long for our secret language. I imagine that I could whisper those words into his ears and I would become more powerful than his homeboys, that the call of our secret language would be more powerful than the call of the streets. But he is no longer three and I am no longer six, and the words we made up are lost forever.

ten

As much as we've made peace with the past, I never stop feeling like I want to make things up to my mother—make up for my brother's failures, for my father's abuse, for the ways each one of us left her. So I buy her things. If I'm shopping and I buy myself a suit, then I'll buy my mother a blouse. I send her vases and candles and antique dolls. One of the first questions I ask when I enter a store is, "Can you ship this somewhere for me?" I'd be a liar if I said my generosity was only about bestowing kindnesses on my mother. It is also about easing my own guilt.

It's been years since I met guys like Ray, who worked in the mailroom at Goldman, Sachs, and felt that we were exactly the same. I am more aware now of how my schooling and experiences separate us. But I cannot get used to the ways in which education and economics separate me from my mother. She is so much a part of me that I half-felt I graduated college for both of us. The newfound abundance of my salary has meaning for both of us. But my mother does not see things this way.

When I was in college, my mother once called me an Oreo—black on the outside, white on the inside. The word, so cruel when it came from my black peers, was like a punch in the face coming from my mother—as if I were a total stranger and not her own child. Later when I told her how much it had hurt me, she said, "But I was just joking!"

Now that I am working, she is fond of calling me a Buppie. I hate it, I tell her, and ask her to stop. But if I talk about wanting to see a certain play or deliberate over whether or not to buy a painting, she can't help but let it slip: "You're such a Buppie." There is a texture of affection and pride in her voice that suggests she's glad I'm not as poor as she was when she was my age, but it is a pride I have trouble absorbing. Her voice says at once, "I am proud of you—but you are now an entirely different being than I am."

Going from poor to middle class was at turns the longest and the shortest transition I have ever made. Long because every day that I went without was just the latest in an unending stretch of days of doing without. Once I'd longed for things so deeply that I kept myself away from malls and shops so as not to preoccupy myself with what I could not have. In college, I collected mail-order catalogues, marking them up with stars and circling the outfits I liked in the colors and sizes I wanted. Desire became a game, and playing the game was satisfying in its own way. At the end of freshman year, a friend asked, "Why do you always mark up those catalogues when you never order anything?" I didn't know he noticed what had become a mindless habit, something I did without thinking. I didn't know what to say. Was he being cruel?

"I don't know," I said, feigning dumbness and vowing to keep the catalogues in my room.

But the jump from poverty to solvency seemed so sudden because it was a jump I made alone. It was just me in an apartment staring at a paycheck that was bigger than any I'd ever seen. Whom could I call, without it sounding like I was bragging? Who wouldn't immediately ask for a loan? Who would understand how a thousand dollars could feel so much like a million? I wanted my mother there on the other end of the phone.

But I also felt guilty, because I felt like she was so much more deserving of that check than I was.

I watched my mother work all her life with no reward greater than a cost-of-living increase. She was always just getting by; in many ways, she still is. I knew that my mother worked hard, but from the example of her life, I knew that hard work was no guarantee of success. Success was only a dream—the big payoff that never came from my father's get-rich-quick schemes or a winning lottery number that came to you in a vision. My life had been different. And even after going to college, after years of hard work, I still felt deep inside that I was more lucky than successful. Like I had dreamed of a number and that number had come in.

∾

A couple of years ago, before my mother moved to Miami, I sent her a gift certificate for a day at Elizabeth Arden as a Mother's Day present. It was the first year I'd earned a good salary and I wanted to do something special for my mother. The gift certificate covered a massage, facial, sauna, and make-over—the works, plus tips. My mother wouldn't have to spend a dime, only the subway token it would take to get her there. I called her up on Mother's Day, all excited about the gift. She was excited, too, and described how it had come gift-wrapped with a big red bow. Then she asked me a question that broke my heart in two. "V?" she whispered. "Do they allow black people in these places?"

It was 1992 and my mother was asking whether Elizabeth Arden would slam the Red Door in her black face.

"Of course they allow black people!" I said, a tone of anger shielding the hurt in my voice. Now I had to be the parent, trying to hide from her the pain and fear in my voice. "I've paid for everything, including a tip for everyone who touches your body. So if one of those bitches so much as looks at you funny, you tell me!"

Months went by and my mother did not use the gift certificate. "You use it," she would tell me. "You work so hard. Burning the candle at both ends. . . ." Finally, I got furious with her and made some empty threat about refusing to talk to her until she went to Elizabeth Arden. She wouldn't budge.

In my frustration I regarded the situation as some sort of Dali-esque fantasy in which I am an avenging angel pushing my mother through the Red Door. When a friend suggested that perhaps my mother did not want to go to Elizabeth Arden alone, I got her neighbor's address and sent her a gift certificate, too. Turns out the woman was just as afraid to go as my mother.

Finally, almost a year later, my mother called me and said, "Guess where I've just been? Elizabeth Arden."

My heart almost stopped. "How was it?" I asked.

"Nice . . . but everyone there was just like you," she said coyly.

"Just like me?" I thought out loud, picturing the Fifth Avenue crowd of older white women laid out on massage tables.

"Professionals. Upper-class women, you know," she replied.

While I was thrilled she went, I wondered just what my mother saw when she looked at me. I wondered if everything that my mother saw as being white about me—my education, my friends, my career—obscured everything that was black about me—my family, my community, my mother. I knew she saw me as different, but it wasn't until she went to Elizabeth Arden that I realized how different.

While there were—and still are—times when I don't feel welcome in certain high-end locations, I know that it is with the bravado of youth and the benefit of my crossover experiences that I either blaze ahead or cop an attitude and leave. My mother believed in the promise of civil rights, but never really thought what those rights would mean to her. She taught us the importance of equality and pride, but she never expected to live in equality herself.

I can see now that beyond the major issues of integration—sitting in the back of the bus, separate water fountains—most of the triumphs of the movement remained for my mother something that happened on t.v. In 1970, my mother gave birth to me and began to work as a secretary. In the 1990s, my mother is still a secretary. She's worked hard all her life, mostly for white people, and the civil rights movement did not change that. What it changed was me and I wasn't some bright young black woman that my mother saw on t.v. I was her daughter. My success brought the benefits of integration through her front door. It was what I had always dreamed of, but it scared my mother. She could call me an Oreo and a Buppie and try to keep what I represented at a safe distance. But the things I bought her, the restaurants I took her to, forced her to consider life differently. Maybe it wouldn't take a winning lottery ticket for her to be able to lead a better life.

I called my mother recently and had a long talk about money. My mother is only forty-five. She has so much life ahead of her. I was hoping that I could use some of what I'd learned about saving and investing to make her life more comfortable. I began to ask her questions: What do your retirement savings look like? What are your financial goals? She had to stop and think.

"You mean goals besides paying the rent and putting dinner on the table?" She laughed nervously.

"Yes," I said. "What do you want to own? What kind of trips do you want to take?"

There wasn't much she wanted to own, although she told me she wanted to start collecting African-American art as I had done. What she really wanted to do was travel. She wanted to go to Jamaica and to Ghana and to Brazil. The tentativeness in her voice was so clear, as if just by saying her wishes aloud, the genie might dive back into its bottle. My mother had never been able to see further ahead than the next day or the next month. I knew then why it scared her when I'd talk about college at ten years old. She didn't know what we were going to eat for the next seven days, much less what she would be able to provide in the way of tuition in seven years.

I told my mother that if she didn't dream, if she didn't think about what she wanted to have, then she was going to wake up and another twenty years would be gone. "There's nothing to save," she said. I asked if I could see her weekly budget. I told her I knew it was personal, but I needed to know exactly how much she and my stepfather made and where it was going. "What budget?" she said.

I wrote down all my mother's figures—how much she owed, what little she had saved, how much she and my stepfather made. I did a budget and a savings plan and I outlined a retirement plan that would give my mother some sort of nest egg for retirement.

"It's not a lot," I told her. "You'll probably still need to work. But maybe you could use it to open a business." I wrote it all out and mailed it to her. When she called me back, I could tell she was impressed. She told me that she and my stepfather had gone over my plan and they thought they could stick to it.

"Where were you twenty years ago?" she asked me jokingly.

"In first grade," I shot back.

My mother told me she had tried to save money when we were little, but often she was too embarrassed to take a five-dollar bill up to the teller's window and deposit it, so she would keep it in an envelope. By the next week, it would be gone.

"Save *change* if you have to," I told her.

"I feel like I can really be hopeful now. Like I have something to look forward to besides bills." Then she paused and added, "I'm still going to play the lottery, and if I hit it, then to hell with your savings plan." I laughed and said that would be fine.

For the first time in my life, I hear in my mother's voice that she is more than just coping, more than just figuring out how to get by. When I hear my mother talk, I can hear her dreaming, and it's the sweetest sound in the world to me.

My mother and I reveal to each other more than we will ever allow anyone else to see. I look at photographs of my mother and my eyes gravitate to the right side of her head. I know that there is a slight scar there. The way the stitches were done, her eyes are slightly uneven. Her right eyebrow is raised slightly and this gives her a look that is at turns quizzical, stern, or outrageously funny. When we go out, I like to make my mother laugh. I save up my best dirty jokes for our visits, I am not above sight gags. My mother's favorite pose for the camera is sticking her tongue way, way out like the Rolling Stones logo. I have more pictures of her tonsils than any loving daughter would need.

When we laugh, I know how far we've come. There was a time when, as a child, I would not know my mother's laugh if I did not see it coming from her mouth. When we laugh now, it is a symbol of our survival, a pat on the back that we give each other for having made it this far. The scars do not go away; we know where they are. The hurt does not go away either. There are bruises that linger underneath the skin that casual acquaintances and even good friends will never see. We have secrets that we keep from each other and that is good, too. But what keeps us close is that we know we will never hurt each other as others have hurt us. Feeling safe together makes our laughter freer—more of a good belly laugh than a polite chuckle or an imperious snicker. Our laughter is honest. In both of our lives, we've made the present better than the past. We don't control the future, but we do have the present. And for now, as often as we can summon it, there is laughter.

VERONICA CHAMBERS is a former editor at *The New York Times Magazine* and *Premiere,* and is currently a contributing editor at *Glamour.* She attended Simon's Rock College at age sixteen and was named one of *Glamour* magazine's Top Ten College Women of 1990. The co-author, with John Singleton, of *Poetic Justice* and a frequent contributor to *Essence, Seventeen, The New York Times Book Review,* and *The Los Angeles Times Book Review,* Chambers has held a Freedom Forum Fellowship at Columbia University. She lives in Brooklyn.